UNCLE SAM IN

EASTERN ENGLAND

From Colonial Times Onwards

Best wishes to Andrew.

Roger Pugh

Norfolk Suffolk Essex
Cambridgeshire
Lincolnshire

ROGER PUGH

Foreword by the Earl of Iveagh

Hodgy Podgy

Books

**Remembering Susan Yaxley
of Larks Press
1937-2016**

Uncle Sam's Roots in Eastern England

is published by
Hodgy Podgy Books,
Thetford, Norfolk
email: hodgy.podgy.books@outlook.com

Designed and printed by
Printing for Pleasure,
Elder House, The Street,
Chattisham, Suffolk IP8 3QE

British Library Cataloguing-in-Publication Data

*A catalogue record for this book is
available from the British Library*

ISBN 978-1-898015-28-4

CONTENTS

Norfolk and Lincolnshire

Suffolk

Finally, the *REAL* Washington . . .

Thanks, Acknowledgements & Sources

FOREWORD

It was in the 1750s and 60s that my Dublin ancestor and namesake, Arthur Guinness, created and established the early popularity of what I am proud to be able to say has become The World's Most Famous Stout.

And it was also in the 1750s and 60s that a young Englishman, Tom Paine, embarked on his career as an unrivalled revolutionary propagandist. Ultimately, Paine went on to write *Common Sense* – in effect, the bible-cum-handbook of the American Revolution or, as we usually call it on this side of the Atlantic, the American War of Independence. He also became the first person to publicly call for the new nation to be named "The United States of America".

What, you may ask, is the connection between these two apparently disparate facts? The answer is that the Guinness family seat, Elveden Hall in Suffolk, lies but a handful of miles from Paine's birthplace of Thetford in Norfolk – a happy proximity which immediately struck members of the United States Air Force when in 1943 my family placed the Hall at their disposal for use as the headquarters of the 3rd Air Division. Inspired by Paine's status as an American hero, the men of the division promptly named a Flying Fortress bomber in the Norfolk man's honour and erected a movingly-worded plaque adjacent to his Thetford birthplace.

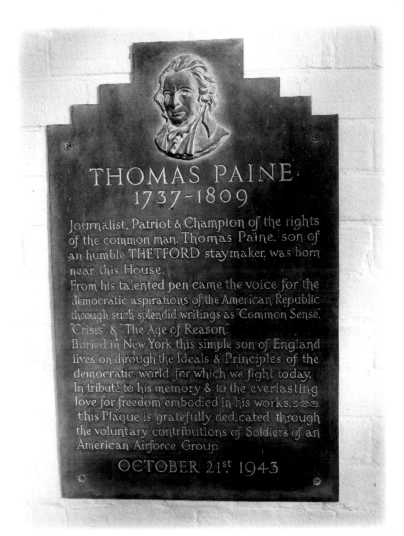

THOMAS PAINE
1737-1809

Journalist, Patriot & Champion of the rights of the common man, Thomas Paine, son of an humble THETFORD staymaker, was born near this House.

From his talented pen came the voice for the democratic aspirations of the American Republic through such splendid writings as "Common Sense", "Crisis" & "The Age of Reason".

Buried in New York this simple son of England lives on through the Ideals & Principles of the democratic world for which we fight today.

In tribute to his memory & to the everlasting love for freedom embodied in his works, this Plaque is gratefully dedicated through the voluntary contributions of Soldiers of an American Airforce Group

OCTOBER 21st 1943

I value highly the historic Second World War friendship between my family and the US Air Force (who during their tenure looked after Elveden Hall with commendable care), and I am confident readers will find Roger Pugh's account of the many other connections between Eastern England and Colonial America & the USA to be as interesting and rewarding as I have done.

Arthur Guinness, Earl of Iveagh

INTRODUCTION

The Grand Union Flag, America's first flag,
raised by George Washington on New Year's Day 1776.
(Artist: Clyde DeLand)

On 3rd December 1775 the founder of the American Navy, Scotsman John Paul Jones, baptised the first American flag by unfurling it on the warship *Alfred* on the Delaware River. Four weeks' later, on 1st January 1776, George Washington ordered his troops to fly it on New Year's Day on Prospect Hill on the fringe of Boston, Massachusetts, where he was besieging the British garrison. Neither of these American revolutionaries saw anything paradoxical in the fact that the upper inner quarter comprised the British Union Flag [1], for the people of the thirteen colonies were almost wholly British by blood and culture; neither were they, at that time at least, committed to throwing off the mother country's yoke – rather, they were looking for what in modern terms might be called Home Rule.

---

1 The Union Flag – or Union Jack – took a slightly different form at the time of the American Revolution: it took its current form in 1801 with the Union of Britain and Ireland.

The new standard so proudly flown by Washington and Jones was – and is – known as 'The Grand Union Flag' (or, sometimes, 'The Continental Colours') and it remained the de facto American national flag throughout 1776 and for much of 1777. The good people of the Somerville area of Boston, Massachusetts remember all this, for they re-enact George Washington's flag-raising ceremony every year; but reports suggest that many, if not most, modern Americans are unaware of this important part of their symbolic history. Neither do the majority of Americans – nor, indeed, the majority of Britons – recall that the tune of the "Star-Spangled Banner" is a rumbustious British drinking song, "To Anacreon in Heaven", written by Englishman John Stafford Smith for a London gentlemen's club in 1773 and later put by the Americans to a rather different use! The thrust of the British lyric was Greek god Anacreon's devotion to women and wine – "I'll instruct you, like me, to entwine/ The myrtle of Venus with Bacchus's wine" – and Smith and his pals much enjoyed singing it at their favourite 'watering hole', the Crown and Anchor pub.

In this book the reader will find many such linkages between the East of England and the United States of America (as it became), from Colonial times onward. Collectively, the five counties of Norfolk, Suffolk, Essex, Cambridgeshire and Lincolnshire played the central role in founding and shaping what is currently the world's most powerful nation. (Though let's admit that they did not always leave Uncle Sam better off – the burning down of the White House and most of governmental Washington in 1814 by the predecessors of today's Royal Anglian Regiment certainly doesn't fall into that category. But the British conquest of the US capital is nevertheless a rattling good yarn and it – and some others like it – are included herein on grounds of balance!)

You can read the book consecutively or in any order you prefer, for each chapter is self-contained. And the great majority of the places mentioned can either be visited or viewed from adjoining land, always with interest and enjoyment. (Naturally, wherever possible check websites in advance and take care to respect private property.)

CAMBRIDGESHIRE & ESSEX

Lordly Lads, Common Convicts and the Lost Colonists of Roanoke

It is early in the year 1587. Many men – and not a few women – lie imprisoned in Colchester Castle, most with little hope of early release. Yet two of these unhappy prisoners, James Hynde and William Clement, are about to experience an uplift of spirit as at last the gaoler opens the postern gate to set them free into the clean Essex air. They breathe it in deeply, a life-affirming contrast to the atmosphere of the filthy cell they have just vacated. Convicted thieves who have served their time, there now lies before them the chance to start life afresh in the New World. Perhaps, at last, they will be able to amass wealth – possibly much wealth – by exchanging careers of petty crime in their homeland for a pioneering existence on the far side of the Atlantic Ocean.

Half-a-day's ride to the north-west, at magnificent Longstowe Hall in Cambridgeshire, two more men, to whom life has dealt a better but not perfect hand, are also breathing in the fresh morning air and feeling shivers of excitement, for they also are about to set off for the New World. Their names are Anthony and John Cage, members of the distinguished family which had built the Hall a decade-and-a-half earlier. They are younger sons, though, not likely to inherit more than a little money and thus needful of making their own way in the world. Where better for them to do so – to gather not only wealth but perhaps also fame – than in Virginia, in a colonisation venture backed by Sir Walter Raleigh, celebrated seaman, adventurer and favourite of the Queen? And what matter if amongst their companions are to be ex-jailbirds such as James Hynde and William Clement – when were pioneers ever anything other than a bunch of 'chancers' of every kind?

Longstowe Hall, the home of the Cage family
(private property)

The one thing that neither the lordly lads nor the common convicts could foresee on the morning of their departure was the fate that *truly* awaited them on the far side of the Atlantic. Had they been soothsayers, they would undoubtedly have changed their minds and remained in England. As it was, they were more than eager to join John White, the man appointed by Raleigh to lead them and 80 or so other men, 17 women and 9 children on a 3,500 mile voyage to Chesapeake Bay in Virginia. No one could have believed that the project would be an easy one, however, for all were well aware that Raleigh's first attempt at promoting a settlement four years earlier, on Roanoke Island off the coast of North Carolina, had ended in failure. Most of the participants in that venture had quickly opted to return to England, leaving only fifteen stout-hearted souls to carry on as best they could.

Out of concern for these fifteen, John White's first task on reaching North American waters this time round would be to anchor briefly at Roanoke to off-load fresh supplies for them or, alternatively, to offer them the opportunity to throw in their lot with the party bound for Chesapeake Bay. Surely, all would go well *there*, for had not Queen Elizabeth commissioned Raleigh to "discover, search, and find out such remote, heathen and barbarous lands, countries and territories . . . to have hold, occupy and enjoy" and to seize and exploit every source of wealth therein? In Chesapeake Bay there would be rich pickings for all, would there not?

Colchester Castle, where the two convicts
Hynde and Clement were imprisoned

So it was that in May of 1587 John White and the other pioneers, including 'our' four, embarked on the *Lion* and two other smaller vessels. The navigator of the little fleet was one Simon Fernandez, a Portugese known to his fellow sailors as the 'Swine', which we may suppose reflected the general view of his character. How or why 'Swine' Fernandez came to be selected for this crucial role we do not know, but a fatal appointment it turned out to be.

Nevertheless, he did get them safely to Roanoke Island, though on landing on 22nd July 1587 White and his party were more than sobered to find that everywhere was deserted. The two-storey, thatched-roof cottages they expected to find had all gone, and the single building still standing was a by-now dilapidated fort. All that remained were some human bones. To their dismay, the new arrivals learned from a nearby group of friendly Native Americans that every one of the fifteen Englishmen they had sought had been slaughtered in an attack by another, more hostile tribe.

After recovering from their shock and disappointment, White and his party became doubly-keen to move on as planned to Chesapeake Bay. But they were stunned yet again when, without the slightest warning, Fernandez announced that under no circumstances would he take them there. "Summer," he declared, "was farre spent, wherefore hee would land all the planters [colonists] in no other place [than Roanoke]". Fernandez' deputy was equally recalcitrant, backing the 'Swine' by bellowing to the rest of the sailors to "leave them [the settlers] behind on the island". Incredibly, Fernandez and his men then proceeded to sail off immediately, abandoning the settlers helpless on shore. Fernandez took the two biggest vessels, leaving White and his people only with the smallest and least seaworthy.

Alone on the vast continent and an ocean away from home, the collapse of the pioneers' plans now stared them in the face. As Anthony and John Cage and ex-convicts Hynde and Clement tried – along with everyone else – to get their minds around what had happened, they must surely have wished they were back in the security of Longstowe Hall or, even, Colchester Gaol, for the outlook had become instantly bleak. The re-supply ships they counted on were unlikely to look for them at Roanoke and their stocks of food and equipment were almost certain to run out long before they could make themselves self-sufficient.

Nevertheless, the new 'planters' – as colonists then were often called – determinedly set about making the best of things, building shelters, repairing the dilapidated fort and preparing to sow crops. Unhappily, they soon lost a number of men to 'Red Indian' attacks and White felt he had no alternative but to lead a reprisal raid. But in a disastrous mistake he attacked the wrong tribe, "killing one and wounding many". As might be expected, this led to a steady deterioration of relationships with all the indigenous peoples except, it seems, the surprisingly amenable Powhatans who lived on Croatoan Island to the south.

By the late summer the settlers had become seriously concerned about their ability even to get through the coming winter. After much discussion it was decided that John White and a small party would re-cross the Atlantic to acquire fresh supplies and, if possible, recruit additional settlers. White was seriously conflicted in his emotions about this: on the one hand, in a bid to save the planters' lives, he felt a duty as leader to risk a dangerous crossing without even a professional navigator for the colony's only remaining and all-too-small boat; on the other hand, his return home would oblige him to leave behind his wife, his daughter and his son-in-law and, poignantly, his newly-born granddaughter, Virginia Dare. (Virginia was the first child to be born of English parents in North America and came into the world a mere nine days before her grandfather departed for England. Her name was chosen "because this childe was the first Christian born in Virginia".) White was also worried that his "stuff and goodes might be spoiled and most of it pilfered away". (Do we here detect fears about the likes of ex-convicts Hynde and Clement?) Finally, he was concerned that his return to the Old World might be seen by Raleigh and others as fleeing to save his own skin. "Much against [my] will", he was eventually persuaded to sail for home.

The return journey for him and his small crew was a terrible one: "Scarce and variable winds" were followed by "a storm at the north-east", a number of sailors were injured and others died of scurvy. Nevertheless, on October 16th 1587 the battered little vessel and its exhausted occupants landed in the west of Ireland, from where White was able to make his way to Southampton. There the poor man was shattered to find that in the light of the threatened invasion of Britain by Spain – which was indeed to come in the shape of the Spanish Armada the following year – Queen Elizabeth I had impounded all shipping for Royal naval use. Initially, not even pleas by Sir Walter Raleigh could persuade 'the Virgin Queen' to release a single vessel to go to the aid of those stranded on Roanoke.

Eventually, White was able to lay his hands on a couple of small pinnaces which were unsuitable for military service but, alas, both were intercepted by French pirates who pounded them with cannon shot, wounded White and "robbed us of all our victuals, powder, weapons and provisions". The journey to Virginia perforce had to be abandoned. White confessed that at this point he became convinced he had been born under "an unlucky star", a conclusion with which we can all surely agree!

Try as they might, Raleigh and White were unable to put together a replacement rescue mission until March 1590 – in other words, not until after a lapse of over thirty months since White's arrival in Ireland. What must he have felt about this delay in terms of concern for the colonists and, above all, for his own family? What of the anxiety experienced at Longstowe Hall back in Cambridgeshire for the two scions of the Cage family? Perhaps some poor souls in Essex even fretted about ex-convicts Hynde and Clements.

Determined still to do his best, from Plymouth White once again set off back to America in command of his little two-vessel fleet, the *Hopewell* and the *Moonlight*. He was surely not surprised to be grievously delayed by more sea battles with French and Spanish privateers and by poor weather. Worse, his eventual landing on Roanoke on August 18th 1590 (his granddaughter's third birthday) became a tragedy in itself, for bad conditions and adverse currents told against him and "seven of the chiefest [mariners] were drowned". The would-be rescuers must surely have hoped that this unhappy sacrifice would at least be mitigated by the joy of reunion with those they had come to help; but no, neither White's family nor any other living soul was to be found. The settlement was, for a second time, utterly deserted.

Buildings had again collapsed and "the houses taken downe". The only real clue to the colonists' fate was the word "CROATAN" carved on a post and the letters "CRO" carved on a tree. Nowhere to be found was the symbol of a Maltese Cross, which it had been agreed would be left by the colonists as a sign if they were taken away by force. What *were* discovered were John White's belongings, which had been buried and hidden, though White found "many of my things [were] spoyled and broken, and my books torn from the covers, the frames of some of pictures and mappes rotten and spoyled with rain, and my armour almost eaten through with rust".

White and his men searched Roanoke and the adjacent islands diligently but to no avail and he and they, consumed with disappointment and regret, returned to Plymouth in England on 24th October 1590. White was to spend the remainder of his life there and at a house he owned in County Cork in Ireland, reflecting constantly, as he put it, on the "evils and unfortunate events" which had devastated his ambitions in the New World. Still clinging obstinately to the hope that somehow, somewhere, his daughter, son-in-law and granddaughter were still alive, he spent much of his remaining time (he was a talented amateur artist) in the melancholy pursuit of painting watercolours of Roanoke scenes.

What *did* happen to the lost colonists? Theories abound but facts are elusive. Some say they left to join the Croatan tribe and were absorbed into their bloodline, others that they were killed either by Native Americans or by rival Spanish settlers, yet others that they simply starved to death. Some say the area suffered a life-destroying drought, others claim to have found traces of the colonists elsewhere, but the fact of the matter is that everything is speculation, nothing – absolutely nothing – has ever been proved.

Probably as reliable as any other hypothesis is the legend that Virginia Dare grew to womanhood in the care of a friendly 'Red Indian' and that her hand in marriage was sought by a handsome young tribal chieftain, only for him to be thwarted by a jealous witch-doctor who turned poor Virginia into a white doe. Some folk claim to have seen the ghost of that white doe haunting the spot where Virginia was born . . . If so, let us hope that, amongst the scene of so much historic tragedy, the white doe is happy at last.

CAMBRIDGESHIRE

The Tavern Keeper's Son Who Founded America's First University

Bull-baiting, bear-baiting, bawdy houses, brawling, boozing and betting are not matters that naturally spring to mind when you stroll amongst the mellow halls, manicured lawns and wooded campus of Harvard, America's first and most famous university. But it was these very things that were the staples of existence in Southwark – one of London's roughest and most disreputable districts – when Harvard University's English founder was born there in 1607.

Though described later in life as a "godly gentleman and lover of learning", John Harvard was the son of a butcher and tavern keeper called Robert Harvard and his wife Katherine. Katherine, seemingly of a somewhat superior social status, hailed from Stratford-upon-Avon in Warwickshire where her father had been a friend of William Shakespeare's father; amongst other things, the two men had served together on the town council. In adulthood Katherine was fortunate enough to inherit some property and by 1627 had accrued an income of her own sufficient to send brainy son John (the fourth of nine children) to Emmanuel College, Cambridge. Emmanuel had been founded 'only' in 1584 and was therefore a relative upstart in a university whose oldest college dated back to 1209. Taking pride in this modernity, Emmanuel had enthusiastically embraced the relatively new-fangled creed of Puritanism. Consequently, John was theologically very comfortable there for, despite (or possibly in reaction to) his origins in sinful Southwark, he was himself a man of marked Puritan disposition. He amply justified his mother's faith in his abilities by earning his Bachelorship of Arts in 1632 and his Mastership in 1635. Academically now well-qualified, he went on to demonstrate his fervent devotion to religion by taking Holy Orders.

*Emmanuel College, Cambridge, the alma mater of
John Harvard, founder of Harvard University*

By 1636, when he married a fellow Puritan called Anne Sadler, he was a man of some wealth, having become, as had his mother, the beneficiary of a number of inheritances. The year following, impelled to seek greater toleration for their religious beliefs, the couple left England and moved to the New World. They settled in Charlestown in South Carolina and John became a freeman. He was also appointed as a teaching elder of the First Church and as an assistant preacher. When he preached and prayed in public, he was so overcome with devotion that he frequently shed "tears of affection strong".

Sadly, his sojourn in America was to be desperately brief, for in September 1638 he died of tuberculosis at the age of 31. However, it was at the time of his death that he took the step that gave him his lasting fame, for he bequeathed £780 (half of his monetary estate) to support a project which had been approved by the Great and General Court of the Massachusetts Bay Colony two years earlier – namely, the founding of "a schoale or colledge" to "advance learning and perpetuate it to posterity: dreading to leave an illiterate ministry to the churches, when our present ministers shall lie in the dust". Having been unable to prepare a written will himself (for the period between the manifestation of his tuberculosis and his death was short), John Harvard perforce dictated his historic wish on his deathbed, his whispered words punctuated by dreadful gasps and struggles for breath.

Harvard House, Stratford-on-Avon, home of
John Harvard's mother as a child and young woman

The Massachusetts Court having previously set aside only a wholly-inadequate £400 for the noble purpose they had envisaged, the Cambridge graduate's legacy of nearly double that sum was consequently pivotal to the project's fulfilment. In addition, he bequeathed his 320-volume scholar's library to the College.

A collection of this size belonging to one person was quite exceptional at that time and it formed the foundation of the fabulous library Harvard University possesses today. In recognition of his crucial role, it was resolved to call the new seat of learning 'Harvard College' and – to reflect the links with Cambridge University, England, which many of the leading colonists had attended – to change the name of its location from Newtown to Cambridge.

At the time of writing Britain's Cambridge is ranked by *The Times Higher Education Supplement* as the fourth-finest university on the planet and Harvard as the sixth. This grave humiliation of currently being 'only' in the top half-dozen of the 4,500 universities that exist world-wide must rankle with both parent and daughter institutions, long-time traditional rivals for first place. No doubt both are now deeply intent on re-establishing their supremacy by deposing the oldest British university, Oxford, from its current ranking as Number One!

CAMBRIDGESHIRE

The Ancestral Home of President 'Silent Cal' Coolidge

In a pleasing contrast to most politicians, Calvin Coolidge, President of the USA from 1923 to 1929, was a man of few words – so few that he eventually became known as Silent Cal. At one high-powered dinner party, a woman sitting next to him said, "I made a bet today that I could get more than two words out of you." Coolidge replied, "You lose". Indeed, the very notion of dinner parties and their compulsory chatter was displeasing to him: asked why he attended them, he said, "Got to eat somewhere". So silent was he generally that on being told he had died, the wit Dorothy Parker inquired, "How can they tell?" Perhaps he inherited this taste for brevity from his father, John, who once replied to an invitation to an important ceremony: "Dear Gentlemen. Can't come. Thank you." Or perhaps there was a genetic strain of verbal hyper-economy in the Coolidge family which stretched all the way back to the President's English ancestors, John and Mary Coolidge of Cottenham in Cambridgeshire.

Cottenham today is a large village about eight miles to the north of Cambridge city. In the early 1600s it was much smaller but then, as now, there stood next to the parish church of All Saints an attractive thatched cottage, as do thatched cottages to this day. The cottage was home to John Coolidge who as a young man was to emigrate to the New World and establish the American branch of the Coolidge family. John was born in September 1604 and in his twenties married a fellow Cottenham resident, Mary Ravens, two years his senior. The couple were Puritans and therefore at odds with the mainstream Anglican Church. Puritanism – the most radical manifestation of dissent – was burgeoning in East Anglia at this time, for Lutheran and Calvinist tenets had flowed in from the European mainland alongside the vessels serving the region's thriving import/ export trade. Indeed, it was this widespread East Anglian adherence to religious dissent – and the consequent attempts at its suppression – that was the principal spur to the region's prominent role in the British colonisation of the New World. In 1628, when John was 24 and Mary 26, Mary gave birth to their first child, a son whom they also named John.

The Coolidge's house in Watertown probably looked very similar to this Watertown dwelling (the Abraham Brown House). Built in the 1600s, it would look equally at home in Cottenham in England. This photo was taken in 1924.

The following year the Puritans and their allies suffered the latest in a series of blows when King Charles I launched a renewed campaign against them. As part of it, the King dismissed from his employment in the Court of Wards and Liveries a Puritan of much greater status than the humble Coolidges, a moneyed man called John

Winthrop, the Lord of the Manor of Groton in Suffolk [2]. In response the miffed Winthrop began to actively contemplate emigration to the New World and, knowing of the existence of the Massachusetts Bay Company, which had already made one or two unsuccessful attempts to establish religious colonies there, he approached its directors. Inspired by their enthusiasm, he became a director himself and played a major part in planning a more ambitious venture, better-financed and better-resourced. The Company accordingly mounted a recruiting campaign for would-be migrants who, like Winthrop, were attracted by the prospect of life in a more congenial religious climate. Eventually a party of some 700 men, women and children, was brought together, amongst them our friends John and Mary Coolidge of Cottenham.

In April 1630 Winthrop, by now the de facto head of the expedition, led the way when he set sail for Massachusetts aboard the Company's flagship *Arbella* in company with three other vessels; these four ships were followed in due course by a further seven. (We do not know which of the eleven carried the Coolidges).

The new colony struggled in its early months, losing in the region of 200 people to a variety of causes, mainly disease. The young Cottenham couple were amongst those who survived and who, like others, were inspired by Winthrop who "fell to work with his own hands, and thereby so encouraged the rest that there was not one idle person to be found in the whole plantation". The Coolidges were allocated thirty acres of land in the settlement of Watertown, now part of the Greater Boston area, and on it they constructed their first American house. Amazingly – and no doubt stemming from the fact that John was a carpenter – they had brought its wooden framework with them from England. The stout Cambridgeshire oak ensured the dwelling's survival into the 1800s (and would have done so for centuries longer, had it not been demolished); it must have looked very similar to dwellings standing in the couple's home village of Cottenham to this day.

---

2 For much more about John Winthrop, see the chapter *The Massachusetts Bay Colony: "The Shining City upon a Hill (or perhaps not . . .)"*

The hard-working John and Mary prospered and in 1636 John was voted a selectman (in modern British terms, a town councillor) of Watertown, a position he was to hold on-and-off for forty years. Church membership was a pre-requisite for this, for the government of the settlement effectively constituted a theocracy – rule, and a stern rule at that, by those who (so they believed) represented God. Over the years, Mary gave birth to eight more children, of whom five survived. John died in May 1691 and Mary a few months later; they could not conceivably have guessed that by founding the American branch of the Coolidge family they would one day bequeath a President to an independent United States.

The family grew and spread and by the 1800s Coolidges were established in Vermont. There, in the town of Plymouth on the auspicious day of the Fourth of July (Independence Day) 1872, the traditionally-named John Coolidge and his wife Victoria welcomed into the world their first child, Calvin, President-to-be. John was a prosperous farmer, storekeeper and minor politician, and he and Victoria were keen that their son be well-educated. In his early years they sent him to a local school and, as he matured, to the Black River and St. Johnsbury Academies. At the age of nineteen he entered prestigious Amherst College (named after British Field Marshall Lord Amherst, a hero of the French and Indian War of 1754-63). There, Coolidge was regarded by his fellows as reserved and reticent but they recognised that he could talk – and talk well – on the rare occasions he wanted to; his class therefore elected him as its speaker and he performed admirably in debates. On leaving Amherst, from which he graduated with honours, he studied law and practiced in the city of Northampton, where he became involved in Republican politics. In 1898 he was elected to the City Council and from there proceeded to climb his way up the political ladder. By 1919 he was Governor of Massachusetts and had established sufficient of a reputation to be nominated by his party for the vice-presidency of the United States in the 1920 elections, Warren Harding being nominated for the presidency itself. The pair were elected but Harding proved to be a grave disappointment, for his time in office was fraught with scandal. Things were unexpectedly brought to an end when he died of natural causes in August 1923, and Calvin Coolidge automatically stepped into the role of President. The news of Harding's death reached Coolidge whilst he was staying with his father in Vermont. He dressed and came downstairs to greet the crowd of journalists which had assembled and his father, who was a notary public, had the deep satisfaction of being able to administer his own son's oath of office in the family parlour. President Coolidge, coolly as you might say, then went back to bed . . .

Coolidge stood in his own right for President in the 1924 election and was elected by a landslide. In his inaugural address, he spoke of problems such as the lynching of black people, child labour and low wages for women but in practice he was to do little or nothing about them. The same can be said of his approach to agriculture where he recognised, but again failed to get to grips with, the problems of poor farmers. His economic policies were relatively simple: he believed in a low-spending government, reduced taxation and in letting business have free rein. He famously said, "The business of America is Business", and in the Roaring Twenties – an exuberant, free-wheeling decade for many, though certainly not for all – Business did indeed serve America well. An era of new cars, new houses, new electrical appliances, jazz music and movie stars, it heralded the onset of modern consumer society. Consequently Coolidge was well-respected by the majority of Americans even if they did not warm to his personality. Surprisingly, given his right-wing views and isolationist-leaning foreign policy (except in relation to South America, where he displayed marked colonialist tendencies), he strongly advocated that the USA should become a member of the World Court, for he was an ardent believer in the rule of law; unfortunately, he was unable to get meaningful legislation through Congress.

Whether or not Coolidge foresaw the disasters of the 1929 Wall Street Crash and the ensuing and world-wide Great Depression we do not know (his wife later maintained he did). But when his term of office was approaching its end and he was on holiday in the Black Hills of Dakota, he unexpectedly issued a laconic statement: "I do not choose to run for President in 1928". Alternative explanations for his decision are that he was still depressed by the death of his son in 1924, or that he no longer relished public life, or that he was unwell – he had certainly taken to sleeping excessively, sometimes for as many as fifteen hours a day, though this might have simply been another manifestation of laid-back Calvin. Be all that as it may, he had said he would not run. And he did not. He died in 1933 at the very modest age of 62, confiding to an old friend shortly before his death, "I feel I no longer fit in with these times".

Whether or not the 30th President of the United States maintains his reputation for brevity in any world there may be beyond ours, we cannot of course know. But if theological discussion forms a part of it, his contributions will be short. On returning from Church on an occasion when Mrs. Coolidge had been unable to attend, she asked, "What was the subject of the sermon?"

"Sin", Coolidge replied.

"And what did the vicar say about it?"

"He was against it."

CAMBRIDGESHIRE

The American Toff Who Saved
His British Enemy's Son

Next only to King George III, the most prominent place on the rebellious colonists' list of hate-figures at the time of the American Revolution was his prime minister, Lord North. Curious it is, therefore, to record that the most profound gratitude Lord North ever expressed to a living being was to a man who signed the American Declaration of Independence.

The man in question, Thomas Nelson, was born in Yorktown, Virginia in 1738, the grandson of an English colonist who amassed a large fortune and for a time served as Governor. The family prided itself that amongst its ancestors was King Edward III, and its links with the home country remained intimate. As was the case with so many other Virginian young men of that era, it was planned to send Thomas to England for the major part of his education. As of 1752, his father did not consider him absolutely ready to cross to the Old World but rapidly changed his mind one Sunday morning. The American writer Harold Titus describes the triggering moment: "Whilst strolling about the outskirts of Yorktown, father Nelson's aristocratic soul was rudely shaken. He had come upon his son playing in the streets with several of the little Negro boys of the village." Appalled, the deeply-prejudiced "Nelson decided quickly that it was time for Thomas to begin his English education. A vessel stood anchored in the harbour ready to sail. Thomas found himself aboard it next the day. He would not return for nine years."

Those nine years in England began with Thomas being placed under the care of a Dr. Newcombe, who ran a school in Hackney, London. On leaving the good Doctor's (to whose care he returned during vacations), he went on to receive the education of a traditional British 'toff', first at that poshest-of-posh British schools, Eton College and then at Christ's College, Cambridge University. 'Toff' is defined by the Cambridge English Dictionary as "a rich person from a high social class" and the Dictionary's publisher, the eponymous University, is surely well-placed to know the truth of this: for in many British eyes there is – or at least, once was – no greater toff than he who boasts the distinction of attendance at both those ancient seats of learning. (Eton College was founded by King Henry VI in 1440 and nestles in rich landscape just across the river from Windsor Castle, the home of English monarchs for nearly a thousand years; whilst 500-year-old Cambridge University, amongst innumerable other royal connections, includes amongst its alumni the pre-eminent 'toff' of the 21st century – Prince Charles, heir to Queen Elizabeth II and the British throne.)

Christ's College, Cambridge,
where Thomas Nelson spent three years

Whilst enjoying Dr. Newcombe's hospitality at Hackney when on vacation from Cambridge (on which occasion we do not know), Thomas performed a noble deed, for he saved from death by drowning the young son of the prominent English aristocrat, Lord North. North was, of course, to go on to be the hated King George III's Prime Minister during the Revolutionary War and second only to the 'Mad King' in the rebel colonists' gallery of villains. North signified his great gratitude to the young Nelson for his brave act by presenting him with a solid-gold snuffbox with a beautifully painted miniature of his lordship on the inside of the lid. We can be sure that Thomas was immensely proud of it (and equally sure that his father would have disapproved of North's encouragement of his son in the pernicious habit of nasally-imbibing pulverised tobacco.)

The Nelson House, Yorktown

When Thomas graduated from Cambridge in 1761, his father – presumably relying on reports from Thomas's tutor, Dr. Porteous – still harboured doubts about his son's behaviour. William even went so far as to cancel the passage he had booked to take Thomas home to America when he discovered that two other aristocratic but disreputable Virginian youths were scheduled to return on the same vessel. (Presumably he vetted the passenger list carefully before booking a replacement ticket!) The reunion of father and son certainly did nothing to assuage Nelson senior's misgivings, for he found Thomas "ate and drank more than was conducive to health and long life". Worst of all, he had taken up smoking "filthy tobacco" – an interesting condemnation from a leading citizen of a colony whose economy flourished on the export of that very crop. Nevertheless, Nelson senior, following good British tradition, was confident that the less-than-perfect Nelson junior was fully-qualified to govern lesser mortals, for in his absence he had entered Thomas's name as a candidate for the House of Burgesses (Virginia's governing assembly). Thomas was duly elected by the obedient voters – one of more than a few examples of Old World-style aristocratic influence still holding sway in the supposedly more-egalitarian New. Shortly thereafter, Thomas married Lucy Grymes and over the years they had eleven children. Parental responsibilities seem not to have cramped his or Lucy's style, however, for the burden of most domestic duties was naturally assigned to some of their 400 black slaves . . .

But over time, despite his royal British ancestry, despite his patrician place in Anglo-American society, despite Eton and Cambridge's best efforts to re-inforce his Anglophilia, Thomas's dominant passion became the pursuit of the thirteen colonies' escape from British rule – a passion no doubt as strong as his continuing belief in his own right to rule those 400 slaves. In 1774 he was elected to represent York County at the first Virginia Convention. He campaigned tirelessly and, delighted by the people of Boston's flamboyant gesture, orchestrated on his local river a Virginian replica of the famous Tea Party. In 1775 he went on to serve in the Second Continental Congress and in the seminal year of 1776 voted for American independence; indeed, 'Thomas Nelson' has the distinction of being one of the 55 signatures on the historic Declaration.

We can see by all this that Thomas firmly rejected his centuries of Royal and English ancestry and his youthful upbringing as a quintessential British toff. But in doing so, did he, as some would say, simply assume the role of an American toff instead? Certainly, his social status played no negligible part in ensuring his appointment as commander of the Militia and his election as Governor of Virginia in 1781. In his military capacity he participated in that same year in the Battle of Yorktown. Thomas's house lay on the battlefield (he was a Yorktown man, remember) and when the British Commander, Lord Cornwallis seized it as his headquarters, Thomas demonstrated his adherence to the cause in an indisputable way, by offering a five guinea reward to any artillery team who could hit it! Unfortunately, ill health forced him to resign as Governor only a few months later, though – much revered by his fellow Virginians – he lived on in retirement in much-reduced financial circumstances.

In considering Thomas Nelson's life it's not inappropriate to end by returning to its greatest irony, his rescue from death by drowning of Lord North's son and the grateful father's gift of the golden snuffbox (which is now in the hands of the Virginia Historical Society). Did Thomas recall the feat to mind when on 4th July 1776 he took up his quill pen to inscribe his name on the Declaration of Independence? And when the official copy of the Declaration later arrived at 10 Downing Street in London, did Prime Minister Lord North think of it when his eyes fell upon Thomas Nelson's signature? It is to be hoped they both dwelt on the event – for a moment at least – for it remains a symbol of man's humanity to man in a world too often characterised by the reverse.

CAMBRIDGESHIRE & SUFFOLK

The Massachusetts Bay Colony – "Shining City
Upon a Hill" (or perhaps not . . .)

John Winthrop was the first governor of the Massachusetts Bay Colony and the leading figure amongst the Puritan founders of New England. It was he who defined the purpose of the colony: *"We shall be as a shining city upon a hill, the eyes of all people are upon us,"* a Biblical quotation which generations of Americans have seen as exemplifying their vision of their country. He is also one of the most illustrious of the alumni of Trinity College of the University of Cambridge.

However, it is as well to state immediately that, as in so many instances in life, Winthrop's stirring rhetoric was more noble than the reality, for he was a denouncer of democracy, describing it as "the meanest and worst of all forms of government" – a fact perhaps unknown to many of his present-day admirers. Additionally, though seeking religious freedom for himself and his adherents, he was strongly intolerant of other religious views, including Anglican, Quaker and Baptist theologies. He was also a firm supporter of slavery, believing that it was authorised by the New Testament: "Slaves, obey your earthly masters with respect and fear, and with sincerity of heart, just as you would obey Christ" (First Epistle of Apostle Peter 2.18). Consequently, many captured Native Americans were enslaved with the approval of the Massachusetts Council, which Winthrop headed. Male warriors, seen as dangerous even in captivity, were shipped to the West Indies whilst women and children were divided amongst the colonists. To quote Winthrop again, the men were traded for "salt, cotton, tobacco and Negroes" – the latter being seen as a lesser threat than the Native American males. This practice

33

Trinity College, Cambridge, where John Winthrop studied

of importing and exporting human beings was to take on the status of an institution, the black 'human imports' and the 'Red Indian exports' condemned alike to lives of abject subjection. Winthrop himself kept three slaves for personal use. Nevertheless, as we shall see, for all his faults, Winthrop was instrumental in placing British North America upon a firm footing.

John Winthrop was born into an intensely religious family in the village of Edwardstone in Suffolk, England in January 1588 and his birth was registered in nearby Groton (later to give its name to the new Groton in Connecticut). In adult life he was to live in Groton Manor, an impressive house dating from the 1450s, and he resided there until his departure for the New World. The house, though subsequently given a Georgian façade, stands to this day and behind the façade the Tudor interior remains. John's father, Adam Winthrop, was a successful and prosperous lawyer and landowner and his mother, Anne, was a landholder too. Initially, the young Winthrop was tutored at home but it is believed he later became a pupil at the Grammar School in Bury St. Edmunds. At the age of fourteen or fifteen, he was admitted to Trinity College, Cambridge, where he made the acquaintance of others who were to have important roles in New England – most notably John Cotton (whose story can be found in the section about Boston and the Pilgrim Fathers). Throughout his life, Winthrop had what he believed were intense experiences of God which, somewhat peculiarly, he described as being akin to conjugal union with Jesus Christ. The young Winthrop, though, was not immune to the attractions of women, confiding to his diary that he felt "lusts so masterly as no good could fasten upon me". These lusts were no doubt assuaged by his marriage at the age of seventeen to an Essex girl called Mary Forth. They were to have five children, though only three survived to adulthood.

Castlings Hall, Groton, where John Winthrop
wooed his second wife, Thomasina Clopton

Groton Manor, Suffolk, John Winthrop's residence

For a while after their wedding Winthrop and Mary lived on her family's lands in Essex but in 1613 Winthrop's father transferred his landholding in Groton to young John, who thus assumed the role of Lord of the Manor there. At about this time he enrolled in Gray's Inn (a legal college) in London to study law but did not pursue the course to the point of qualifying as a lawyer. Instead, he returned home to Groton to assume civic duties and carve out for himself a role as a religious leader. His marriage to Mary ended with her death in 1615 but he re-married quickly, to a lady called Thomasina Clopton, who was herself sadly to die only a year later from childbirth complications (the baby dying with her). Never one to be without a woman for long, within months Winthrop married for a third time, to Margaret Tyndal, who came from a prosperous Puritan and legal family, and this final marriage proved to be long and loving.

The area Winthrop had been brought up in was one he had perceived as a youth to be Godly, but as time elapsed a local decline in the numbers of those who shared his views (despite his best efforts at evangelism), together with the appointment of anti-Puritan bishops in London and Norwich, left him feeling alienated. He dabbled with the idea of moving to Ireland, ultimately deciding against, and at about the same time found himself involved in legal disputes about his inheritance. Though continuing to participate in public life, including assisting in drafting of bills for Parliament (notably against drunkenness – surely then, as now, a largely lost cause) he concluded that true religion – *his* religion – could no longer be satisfactorily pursued in his native land.

In 1629 he joined the Massachusetts Bay Company, a group of investors who wished to establish a colony in the New World and had been authorised to do so by the King, Charles I. Winthrop and a group of like-thinking fellow Puritans soon succeeded in taking over control of the Company, their ambition being to establish a Puritan community, though not without regard to the realities of money and power. The area available for settlement was vast, stretching from the Merrimac to the Charles Rivers. In April 1630, accompanied by his two young sons Samuel and Stephen, Winthrop set sail from Southampton on the *Arbella*, one of several vessels carrying in all about 700 emigrants. They arrived in Salem, Massachusetts in July but found it inadequate as a place to accommodate all the arriving colonists. They then flirted with moving to Charlestown but, finding the water supplies there insufficient, they moved on and founded what is today the city of Boston.

Elected as first Governor of the Massachusetts Bay Colony by a coterie of a mere eight men, who thus put themselves in flagrant breach of the more democratically-nuanced Charter granted them by the King, Winthrop and his fellow churchmen immediately established what in substance was a theocratic semi-dictatorship. No-one but church members were recognised as freemen, and no-one but a freeman was permitted to vote or hold office. This handy arrangement was further buttressed by the appointment of the Massachusetts Bay Company's officers as the sole magistrates, and these same magistrates dispensed rulings in accordance with the dogma pronounced by the Church leaders. In short, the entire set-up was a nicely circular way of ensuring rigid obedience. Those who *did* rebel were promptly suppressed or banished. (It is curious that so many of the New World pioneers, much revered by succeeding generations, were of totalitarian disposition in a land which today prides itself on its democracy. In Winthrop's case, it cannot even be claimed that he intended his 'shining city upon a hill' to offer a decent life to the common man: "In all times", he said, "some must be rich, some poore, some highe and eminent in power and dignitie; others mean and in subjection". So much for the American Dream!)

None of this was to stop the colony from flourishing, however, with some 20,000 British immigrants arriving in the 1630s alone, fleeing either for religious reasons or (despite Winthrop's assertion of some always being "mean and in subjection") in the largely-correct belief that they would ultimately establish more prosperous or congenial lives there than in their native land. Much of this progress was undoubtedly attributable to Winthrop's great gifts as an administrator and to his willingness to set a personal example of hard work and settlement-building. He joined servants and labourers in the physical development of the colony and, it is recorded, "fell to work with his own hands and thereby so encouraged the rest that there was not an idle person to be found in the whole plantation". He still found time for petty disputes, however: for example, he fell out with Thomas Dudley, the chief magistrate, over what he considered to be the excessively decorative woodwork in Dudley's house, excessive decoration apparently being an affront to the Lord.

Other disputes had more serious causes, prime examples being the cases of fellow settlers Anne Hutchinson and John Wheelwright, who believed that departing from religious laws did not necessarily and irretrievably bar a person from salvation – the so-called Antinoniam heresy. The colony bitterly divided over the matter and in 1636 Hutchinson and Wheelwright were put on trial and banished. This did not unduly set them back, for Hutchinson soon founded Portsmouth, Rhode Island and Wheelwright established Exeter, New Hampshire and then Wells, Maine, where they flourished free of Massachusetts rule. [3]

---

3 An account of Anne Hutchinson's tragic fate is to be found in the chapter *The First Governor of America's Smallest State and Persecutor of "The Woman More Bold Than a Man"*

Despite the fact that theological disputes of various kinds forever rumbled, the colony's religious fervour was diluted by the arrival in ever-growing numbers of those less committed to a hard line than were the original settlers. Nevertheless, this did not stop the Massachusetts Body of Liberties of 1641 from stipulating that "if any man after legal conviction shall have or worship any other god but the Lord God, he shall be put to death" – a sentiment to which, of course, 21st century ISIS also fervently subscribes.

And as late as 1684, the perennial Puritan question of the sinfulness or otherwise of dancing was still inflaming debate. The influential New England minister Coton Mather wrote: "Concerning the controversy about Dancing, the Question is not whether all Dancing be in itself sinful . . . Nor is the question whether a sober or grave Dancing of Men with Men, or of Women with Women be not allowable . . . But our question is concerning Gynecandrical Dancing, or that which is commonly called Mixt or promiscuous Dancing, viz. of Men and Women (be they elder or younger persons) together. *Now this we affirm to be utterly unlawful, and that it cannot be tolerated in such a place as New England without great sin*". (Mather's original emphasis.) One is reminded of the old joke about members of the Scottish Presbyterian Church: "They are much against sex because sex can lead to dancing . . ."

But let us leave all that aside, however ludicrous or distasteful much Puritan thought was, and conclude by remembering that under John Winthrop's longstanding leadership, Massachusetts established itself firmly, went on to flourish, and, many years after his death, took the leading part in initiating the American Revolution. Despite all his narrowness, for forging the first links in this chain John Winthrop must be granted massive recognition.

CAMBRIDGESHIRE

Harley-Davidson Motorbikes

Milwaukee, Wisconsin, USA takes the credit for manufacturing those big, heavyweight, iconic, chrome-laden, glitzy, often whitewall-tyred and sometimes leather-fringed motorbikes which emit a characteristic thumping noise that's inspired generations of bikers. ("Turn on your own thunder", as the advertisement says.)

or

Milwaukee, Wisconsin, USA must take the blame for manufacturing adolescently-brash, mechanically-backward, 'self-propelled public relations machines' with a thumping and thudding decibel output that destroys normal people's nerves. ("A Harley-Davidson is the most efficient way to convert gasoline into noise, without the side-effects of horsepower").

Well, you pays your money, a lot of it for a Harley, and takes your choice but, whichever your choice is, it's not Milwaukee but rather the small town of Littleport in Cambridgeshire, England that merits the praise or blame for the existence of 'Hogs' as they're fondly known by their *aficionados*. (From the acronym for **H**arley **O**wners' **G**roup). For it was in Littleport in 1835, in a cottage in Victoria Street, that a man called William Harley was born. His wife was called Mary and in 1860 the couple emigrated to the United States. Soon after their arrival, William participated in the American Civil War on the Union side as a soldier in the New York Heavy Artillery. Surviving the conflict, Arthur fathered several children, one of whom was William Sylvester Harvey, who took his first breath in 1880. It was this William Sylvester Harvey, of pure British blood, who was to found Harley-Davidson Inc. in 1903. He was helped by his childhood friend, Arthur Davidson, another young man of pure British blood, for Arthur's father had emigrated from Scotland and married a Scots girl, Margaret McFarlane, who lived in the small Scottish settlement of Cambridge, Wisconsin.

By the turn of the nineteenth and twentieth centuries, the craze for pedal-bikes was sweeping the United States. Motorbikes were catching on too, for by then they were already popular in Britain and Germany. Famously, the first-ever motor car had been produced by Germany's Karl Benz in 1888 and it was Germany which pioneered the motorcycle, too – notably with the Hildebrand and Wolfmuller 'Motorrad' of 1894 – though Britain was not far behind.

Knowing all this, in 1901 the 21-year-old British-blooded William Sylvester Harley was seized with the ambition of producing his own indigenous American machine. Thus inspired, he set about designing a small (a *very* small) engine of 116cc, or just over 7 cubic inches, for installation in a conventional pedal bicycle frame. With help from the aforesaid Arthur Davidson and Arthur's two brothers, Walter and William, over the next two years he succeeded in putting together a prototype. Sadly, on testing it proved a flop, for it hadn't enough power to climb even a small incline without pedal assistance – a searing disappointment because, of course, the whole point of fitting the bike with an engine was to eliminate physical effort and to radically enhance speed and range. The team thus had no choice but to write off their first effort to experience – and indeed they *had* learned much, albeit at a cost.

They had also learned the value of perseverance and so, undaunted, they set about work on a second machine. This they fitted with an engine over three times as big, designed with help from Swedish-born Ole Evinrude, whose name is nowadays indelibly associated with the famous outboard motors. They designed and constructed a new and custom-made frame, too, and put the whole machine together in the Davidson family backyard, some of its parts having been manufactured, possibly illicitly, in the West Milwaukee railroad workshops where Walter was a machinist. In September 1904 the new model came fourth in a race at the Milwaukee State Fair, and in 1905 the new little company began selling its engines to other motorbike producers. It also sold three of the five complete bikes it manufactured that year. "From acorns, oak trees grow. . ."

The classic image of a Harley-Davidson as most people think of them (Note disabled person's parking badge- few things stop a 'Hog' rider, apparently!)

The enterprise expanded rapidly and in 1906 the friends built the first Harley-Davidson factory on Juneau Avenue, Milwaukee, where the company's headquarters remain to this day. Sales boomed and in 1914 production reached 16,284 machines. Massive numbers were sold for military use after America entered the First World War in 1917, and by that time the company could rightly consider itself one of the USA's most successful companies.

A decade or so later, however, the Great Depression hit Harley-Davidson desperately hard and output slumped from 21,000 in 1929 to 3,700 in 1933. But the company survived and flourishes to this day in the manufacture of highly-distinctive machines, of which it now sells in excess of a quarter-million a year. Most are powered by very large engines, possibly in psychological reaction to a company 'folk memory' of William's disastrously-puny first motor!

The author's wife at the memorial to the founder of
Harley-Davidson motorbikes, Littleport, Cambridgeshire

We must conclude by recording that though Harley-Davidsons are viewed in some quarters as not being the epitome of technical sophistication or elegance in appearance, their proud owners just *know* that their magnificent machines are *unrivalled*, that their brilliant bikes have *soul*! But of one thing we can *all* be certain: that the British-originated company will continue to recruit many more generations of devoted 'Hog' lovers, of whom more than a few will make pilgrimages to their Holy Grail, that small town of Littleport, Cambridgeshire, just as they do today.

ESSEX

A British Officer in the American Civil War 1861-1865

Fighting the Native Americans, fighting the Spanish, fighting the French, fighting the Dutch, fighting their own kith and kin in the American Revolution, fighting yet again against the independent United States in the War of 1812: you might have thought that the British would have had enough of spilling blood and having their own blood spilled in North America. But no, still keen to have another go, over 50,000 British citizens participated in the American Civil War of 1861 to 1865. Some fought out of sympathy for the anti-slavery cause of the Union side, some (many fewer) out of sympathy for the Confederacy; yet others volunteered simply from a sense of adventure or to slake the thirst for battle aroused in them by fighting for Queen and Empire against the Russians in the bitter, recently-concluded Crimean War.

Amongst the 50,000 Britons were numerous generals and an astonishing 71 winners of the Medal of Honour (the US equivalent of the British Victoria Cross, the country's highest award for valour). We shall take as representative of this great host the story of an Essex man, Major John Carwardine, the son of the Reverend Carwardine, Rector of Earls Colne, a village lying thirty or so miles west of the county town of Colchester. John Carwardine's uncle was Lord of the Manor of Earls Colne and so the family was one of considerable local influence. Carwardine had joined the British Army as a young man but in 1861, at the age of thirty-three, he decided to cross the Atlantic and fight for Abraham Lincoln and the Union. He was soon commissioned as a captain in F Company of the 6th New York Cavalry, which was part of Major General George B. McClennan's Army of the Potomac.

Earls Colne Priory, Essex,
John Carwardine's home

In mid-October 1861 Carwardine, who had been rapidly promoted to the rank of major, was part of a Union expeditionary force of 400 men commanded by Colonel John Geary which crossed the river at Harpers Ferry in West Virginia. It was a much-contested place, changing hands no fewer than fourteen times during the course of the war. One long-suffering resident recalled: "When the Union army came they called the citizens Rebels – when the Confederates came they called them Yankees". But the warring parties did agree on two things. First, a shared dislike of the town: the soldiers generally described it as "a god-forsaken, stinking hole". Second, a shared respect for the British flag, for a resourceful Irish priest, Father Michael Costello, ensured his church of St. Peter remained unscathed throughout by flying the Union Jack from its steeple. The symbol of neutrality was respected by both sides (remember, all Ireland was part of the UK at the time) and under the supervision of a fellow Irishman, Dr. Nicholas Marmion, the church was used as a hospital serving wounded Unionist and Confederates alike. And Father Costello kept up his schedule of services, too!

John Carwardine in his uniform as a Union officer

At the time of Colonel Geary's arrival there was anxiety on the Union side that the area might be used by the rebels as a staging post for an attack on Washington and Geary's move was an anticipatory, defensive one. He did indeed find Confederate troops strongly posted on the neighbouring 1.000 foot heights and in the vicinity of Charlestown but no immediate conflict ensued. However, on the 20th of the month the Confederates made a determined attempt to repel Geary's men, launching an attack with substantial numbers of cavalry and infantry supported by a heavy bombardment from the artillery pieces on the heights. After some skirmishing Geary's men charged and succeeded in compelling the whole rebel force to retire. The official despatch of the 6th New Yorkers recorded: "The advance, under Lieutenant-Colonel McVicar and Major Carwardine . . . charged the main body and routed them completely". Geary himself summed up matters thus: "Our cavalry exhibited much bravery in their charge and conducted themselves throughout admirably. Col.

Devlin, their commander, Lt. Col. McVicar and Major Carwardine are deserving of much approbation for their display of gallantry and ability". (The engagement proved to be the preliminary to a much larger one fought the following day which goes under the name of the Battle of Ball's Bluff. The 6th New York Cavalry are not listed in the order of battle for this latter clash. Things might have gone better for the Union side had they been, for the Confederates scored a resounding victory. The humiliation of the Union force was so great that an alarmed Congress set up a special commission to review and regulate the conduct of the war.)

John Carwardine continued to serve the Union with distinction in more than a few fights until 1863 when some sort of problem arose at home which necessitated his return to England, for in March of that year he wrote to the New York headquarters of his unit, "It being expedient that I should visit my home in England on business of some importance, I hereby tender my resignation and respectfully request an honourable discharge from the service of the United States". This, of course, was granted, accompanied by an expression of deep appreciation for his assistance to the Union. Later, John Carwardine married the daughter of a Cumberland Justice of the Peace and inherited his family's estate at Earls Colne.

In a wider context, one must record that the American Civil War divided not only the USA but Britain, too. The British upper classes tended to favour the Confederacy, the public at large to favour the Union, but this split of opinion was by no means hard-and-fast. Certain it is, though, that the Confederacy was able to hold out as long as it did only because, as historian Peter Tsouras has put it, "the output of British factories, mills, shipyards and arsenals flooded through the Union blockade to provide the bulk of Confederate needs. Without that massive support, the Confederacy would surely have collapsed within 12 to 18 months." A warship called the *Alabama* which the British built for the Confederate Navy, and whose crew members, too, were almost all British, took on a totemic role as the symbol of the support by the Old Country for the breakaway states, and was even cited in a court case in New York as a reason for not complying with a request from London for the extradition of a British man suspected of murder who had fled to the USA. The alleged murderer's defence counsel contended that in effect a state of war existed between Britain and the United States and that this abrogated all treaties between the two nations: "England cannot say she is neutral . . . when she furnishes our rebellious subjects with vessels of war, mans them, opens her ports to them, furnishes them with arms and ammunition and sends them forth on errands of destruction, burning merchant ships and destroying the commerce on the seas of a friendly power. The *Alabama*, built and armed in England, and manned by Englishmen, sank and burned one hundred and twenty of our ships . . ." [4]

A prime British motive behind assisting the Confederates was, of course, the acquisition of profit – or, perhaps more accurately, the minimisation of loss, for traditional trade with the Confederacy had perforce declined by 90% from its pre-war levels. Crucially, this had crippled the massive and highly-profitable North-of-England cotton-manufacturing industry, for it was from the Confederate states that the great bulk of its raw material had come. Absence of cotton meant absence of jobs, and huge numbers of men, women and children who had been amongst Britain's most prosperous were thrown into extreme poverty. Despite this they strongly and steadily supported the Union and made that support crystal-clear. For example, the inhabitants of Manchester passed a resolution of support which they sent to President Lincoln. He replied, "I know and deeply deplore the sufferings which the working people of Manchester . . . are called to endure in this crisis . . . Under the circumstances I cannot but regard your decisive utterances on the question as an instance of sublime Christian heroism which has not been surpassed in any age or any country . . . whatever else may happen, whatever misfortune may befall your country or my own, the peace and friendship which now exists between the two nations will be, as it shall be my desire to make them, perpetual." The good people of Manchester went on to erect a statue of Lincoln in the city with a quotation from his letter inscribed on the plinth.

---

4 The judge, whatever his personal feelings, was not persuaded by the argument and confirmed the legal validity of the request. After a massive run of success, the worn-out *Alabama* was eventually sunk.

Of course, life is never quite as heart-warming as Lincoln's noble hope, and the British role in the American Civil War was in fact to sour relations between the two countries for many a year. But, thankfully, friendship was to be renewed and more than that, firmly cemented, by the later example of men such as Theodore Roosevelt and the Prince of Wales, descendant of America's bete noire, King George III . . .

After his return to his home in Earls Colne, Major John Carwardine, Unionist supporter par excellence, must have observed events in the United States and in his own country with continuing fascination but, sadly, he was to die of throat cancer at the relatively early age of 62. When, decent man that he was, he became aware that his days were numbered, he visited every worker on his estate to say goodbye and presented each of them with a gold sovereign. He has no commemorative statue but his Essex home still stands to symbolise the life of this man of courage and principle and the 50,000 other British citizens who put themselves in danger on the far side of the Atlantic Ocean to fight for what they believed was right.

His grave is in Earl Colne's churchyard.

ESSEX

William Penn and the Founding of Pennsylvania

There was a slight delay in granting American citizenship to the man who founded the State of Pennsylvania – a little matter of over 300 years. For it was not until 1984 that President Ronald Reagan, authorised by a resolution of Congress, made a Proclamation conferring that status on one-time Essex schoolboy William Penn, who as an adult English Quaker left the Old World for the New in 1682. But when formal recognition came at last, it was fulsome:

"In the history of this Nation there has been a small number of men and women whose contributions to its traditions of freedom, justice and individual rights have accorded them a special place of honour in our hearts and minds, and to whom all Americans owe a lasting debt. Among them are the men and women who founded the thirteen colonies that became the United States of America.

William Penn, as a British citizen, founded the Commonwealth of Pennsylvania in order to carry out an experiment based upon representative government; public education without regard to race, creed, sex, or ability to pay; and the substitution of workhouses for prisons. He had a Quaker's deep faith in divine guidance, and as the leader of the new colony he worked to protect rights of personal conscience and freedom of religion. The principles of religious freedom he espoused helped to lay the groundwork for the First Amendment of our Constitution.

As a man of peace, William Penn was conscientiously opposed to war as a means of settling international disputes and worked towards its elimination by proposing the establishment of a Parliament of nations, not unlike the present-day United Nations."

President Reagan also conferred the honour of citizenship on William Penn's wife, Hannah:

"[Hannah Penn] effectively administered the province of Pennsylvania for six years and, like her husband, devoted her life to the pursuit of peace and justice."

William Penn was born at Tower Hill, London in 1644, the son of a 23-year-old Captain in the Royal Navy (who was later to be knighted and reach the rank of Admiral) and his wife Margaret. The family had the distinction of being neighbours of the world's most famous (and amorous) diarist, Samuel Pepys, who was disappointed in his attempt to seduce William's teenage sister Peggy – an uncharacteristic failure. One might add that William's mother Margaret might also have been one of Pepys' targets (and an easier one, for she was a playful lady) had her looks been a little less faded, for she once flung "Pepys on a bed at a party and heaped female guests upon him".

As an adult, William Penn was to lay much emphasis on the importance of bringing up youngsters responsibly, declaring that "men are generally more careful of the breed of their horses and dogs than of their children". This is a view he presumably inherited from his father, who sent him to be educated for three years (from 1655 to 1658) at the highly reputable Chigwell Grammar School in Essex. School Archivist Marian Delfgou tells us that in Penn's day the school buildings comprised the Tudor Guildhouse, the so-called 'Big School' classroom (now the Swallow Library) and Harsnetts House across the lane. She goes on: "Water came from wells . . . light from rush-lights and candles, warmth and hot food from the big fireplaces and food for the mind from Latin Master Edward Cotton who flogged his boys and taught them by rote. Books were still rare and expensive and so learning by repetition was usual. William Penn and his fellow scholars would have repeated declensions, learned Cicero and Caesar and struggled with goose-quills and soot-black ink to scratch out their Latin and Greek grammar and histories . . . There was little arithmetic."

Chigwell School, Essex, still flourishing in the 21ˢᵗ century. Here, Penn had his first religious experience.

It was at the school that the eleven-year-old William had his first religious experience. His friend, John Aubrey, recorded that when alone in his room there, the boy "was so suddenly surprized with an inward comfort and (as he thought) an externall glory in the roome that he has many times sayd that from thence on he had the sense of divinity and immortality . . ."

Later the whole Penn family, including William, moved to Macroom in Ireland where Penn senior was sent to help suppress dissident Roman Catholics. Here they came into contact with Thomas Loe, a noted Quaker preacher who impressed the precocious William greatly. Essentially, the Quakerism which Loe preached was and is the collection of beliefs and practices developed by George Fox who, in 1647, became convinced that all who so desired could have a personal experience of God – Fox's definition of God being 'Inner

Light'. No mediation by a priest was required, Fox said, and worship could be conducted by believers gathering together and meditating in silence unless and until one or other was moved to speak of his or her thoughts or insights. Fox travelled widely, preaching to whoever would listen, urging his hearers to become 'Friends of the Light' – the 'Friends' element ultimately morphing into the formal title of the movement, 'The Society of Friends'. The informal or popular terms, 'Quakers' and 'Quakerism', arose from an occasion when Fox was charged with blasphemy: one of the magistrates, Fox wrote in his autobiography, "was the first that called us Quakers, because I bade them tremble at the word of the Lord".

In 1660 at the age of sixteen, the Quaker-leaning William left Essex and was sent to Oxford University. There he soon came into conflict with the authorities at his college, Christ Church, for holding 'silent' services in his room instead of attending chapel. Ultimately they expelled him for his continued theological disobedience, for which 'crime' he received a good beating from his father, who had *not* been impressed by Fox's apostle, Loe, and to whom Quakerism was just as abhorrent as it was to the University hierarchy. A period followed in which the recalcitrant young man was sent on the almost-compulsory Grand Tour of Europe, where he picked up a taste for stylish and expensive clothing, a pardonable indulgence. On his return he studied law and spent further time in Ireland, where he helped his father put down another Catholic rebellion. He proved himself not short of courage in battle and was proud enough of his efforts to commission a portrait of himself in armour. This was curious, for he was later to develop a profound detestation of violence, and pacifism was to become an absolute and un-negotiable tenet of Quaker belief.

Significantly, at the age 24 William discussed with a friend, Josiah Cole, the possibility of establishing a 'utopia' – an ideal nation – in British America, a land from which Cole had recently returned. At about this time, too, William came into personal contact with Quakerism's founder, George Fox, and it is not a surprise that his commitment to, and prominence in, the movement became still greater. Nor is it a surprise that in 1670 he and a fellow-believer

(William Mead, a former captain in Cromwell's army) were arrested for preaching the heretical Quaker doctrine in the streets of London and thrown into Newgate Prison. It was not a pleasant place. Charles Dickens knew the prison and in his novel *Moll Flanders* puts a description of it into the mouth of the eponymous Moll: "The hellish noise, the roaring, swearing and clamour, the stench and nastiness, and all the crowd of afflicting things that I saw there, joined together to make the place seem an emblem of hell itself and a kind of entrance into it". There the accused pair awaited their trial, at which no less a person than the Lord Mayor of London, Sir Samuel Starling, was to preside.

Court proceedings commenced with a battle of wills between the two defendants and Sir Samuel over the question of their hats, which Penn and Mead refused to doff to him, for as Quakers they held that all people were equal and hat-doffing would imply a recognition of his superiority. The defendants won this initial skirmish, and Penn went on to fight the case eloquently and point-by-point – indeed, so successfully that the members of the jury returned a verdict of not guilty. The angry Sir Samuel ordered them to think again and an epic struggle ensued, the jury being confined without food, water or even a chamber-pot for three days. During this period the Lord Mayor ordered them on four occasions to reverse their verdict. However, the twelve 'good men and true' stuck to their guns. This left the by-now apoplectic Sir Samuel helpless to do anything other than seek revenge, which he achieved by fining each and every juror for contempt of court, and by sending Penn and Mead to prison for their refusal to remove their hats! One juryman, Edward Bushell, resolutely declined to pay, despite being rich enough to cover not only his own fine but those of the others too; instead, he chose to submit himself to joining Penn and Mead in Newgate. Eventually the valiant Bushell, whose name shines in the history of Anglo-Saxon jurisprudence, was successful in obtaining his freedom after applying for a writ of Habeus Corpus, thus establishing the historic right of British (and subsequently American) juries to reach their verdicts without Government interference. The two Quakers were eventually released, too.

While the court case was in process, Admiral Penn died and despite earlier threats to disinherit William, left him a yearly income of £1,500 (£230,000 in terms of purchasing power in 2017). Thus, William Penn suddenly became a very rich man. Over the next decade, freed from any concern about money, he continued to preach, write and from time to time appear in court charged with this, that or the other religious offence. His dream of a 'utopia' in the New World continued throughout and in 1681 it culminated in decisive action when, in response to lobbying by him, King Charles II signed over to him a vast tract of American land to which the monarch gave the name Pennsylvania in honour of his father, the Admiral. At this time, its population barely exceeded three thousand.

William effectively became the sovereign of this new domain, its owner and governor, free to draft its constitution and make its laws as he himself desired. This would have tempted many a man to establish his own vast fiefdom and to ensure its government, religion and society were run according to his diktats. In a sense, one can say that everything *was* run in accordance with his diktats, for they were diktats of equality, liberty and freedom of religious belief. Penn's concept of equality even extended to the Native Americans: "Be tender of offending the Indians . . . to soften them to me and the people, let them know you are come to sit down lovingly with them . . . be grave, they like not to be smiled on". On another occasion he said, "Let them have justice and you win them".

In terms of theology, William demonstrated an unusual, if not unique, tolerance: many a man and woman had emigrated to the New World in pursuit of religious freedom, yes, but all too often the religious freedom they sought was for themselves and themselves alone; their intolerance and frequent persecution of others all too often bore the hallmarks of what they claimed to abhor. Amongst them, William Penn shone out as a bright light in darkness by virtue of meaning what he said.

Keen, too, to promote healthy and pleasant ways of life, William took a close personal interest in the planning of the capital, Philadelphia, which was to feature "gardens or orchards or fields, that it may be a green country town, which will never be burnt and always be wholesome". In this his ambitions long foreshadowed the establishment of Bourneville in England 200 or more years later by those other benign Quakers, the Cadbury family.

The enlightened constitution of Pennsylvania appealed to many, not only Quakers, and the population grew rapidly, with farming, housing and schooling all making commensurate progress. However, back in England the persecution of the Friends continued apace and in 1684, having ensured Pennsylvania's solid foundation, William returned to his home country to see what he could do to help. Five months after his return, the sympathetic King James II came to the throne and William was able to persuade him to release 1,300 Quakers from prison – valuable help indeed. However, not all went well with William personally, for when King James II was overthrown a few years' later by King William III, William was thrown into gaol for continuing to correspond with the now-exiled James. This culminated with William being charged with treason in 1692, though he was eventually exonerated.

Whilst William was in England, others administered Pennsylvania on a day-to-day basis on his behalf but his commitment to the territory did not falter, as exemplified by his contributing £3,000 more to its finances during this period than he received in income from his holdings there. In 1699 he returned to Pennsylvania and encouraged the freeing of black slaves whom he discovered had been imported. But largely through his generosity, and despite having been a very wealthy man, he was by this time severely indebted, having in all contributed £20,000 to the coffers of the by-now flourishing territory. His financial difficulties lingered on, culminating in his arrest for debt in 1708 on a summons issued by, sadly, fellow Quakers from Bristol, England, who foreclosed on a loan. But such was the affection and regard in which he was held by Pennsylvanians that in 1710 the House of Assembly granted him sufficient monies to alleviate his distress and to enable him to live a modest life.

Unhappily, a mere twenty-four months' later he was struck by paralysis and his memory was deeply impaired. After six trying years, during which wife Hannah ably administered Pennsylvania on his behalf, he died, his body being returned to his native land for burial at Jordans in Buckinghamshire.

William Penn remains remarkable not only for all the reasons enumerated in President Reagan's proclamation but for these additional reasons too: he was that highly unusual human being, a man who meant what he said, acted as he counselled others to act (as was not the case with many of America's founders) and truly did leave the world a better place than he had found it. Let us hope, therefore, that the good William rests forever in the peace that he and all other Quakers value so very much.

ESSEX

George Washington: The Descendant of a "Scandalous and Malignant Priest"

George Washington is probably the most famous name in American history, for he it was who led the British colonies in their struggle to free themselves from their motherland and went on to became the first President of a new nation, the United States of America. He has been described by The Los Angeles Times as "the last Englishman and the first American", and in his lifetime was known as "the father of his country".

The great man's family line in northern England can be traced as far back as the 12th century. His immediate English ancestors, however, came from the eastern county of Essex and focus on a "scandalous and malignant priest", the Reverend Lawrence Washington of Purleigh and, later, Little Braxted. It was three of this "scandalous and malignant" priest's offspring who were to emigrate to Virginia between the 1650s and 1670s and establish the colonial branch of the family which was to produce the famous George.

Lawrence Washington – also described as "a common frequenter of alehouses" who "encouraged others in that beastly vice'"–had been born in 1602 in Sulgrave Manor in Northamptonshire. Purchased in 1539 by an even earlier Washington, it survives to this day, its stonework now gloriously mellowed by the passage of time. It lies about a hundred miles west of the aforesaid Essex villages to which Lawrence was later to move and live in for the greater and most important part of his adult life.

At the time Lawrence was born there was still money in the Washington family, though as a fifth son he could not have expected much of it to come his way, and indeed it did not. Consequently, education for a career was essential and at the age of 17 he entered Brasenose College at Oxford University and graduated as a Bachelor of Arts in 1623. He seems to have been well-regarded by the College authorities, for only a few days after graduation he was elected as a Fellow, the first step on the ladder to higher office in the Church. He became a Master of Arts in 1626 and twelve months after that was appointed as Lector, the chief disciplinarian of the College's often-unruly undergraduates, a somewhat ironic appointment in view of his own reputation in later life. In 1631 the Chancellor of the University, William Laud, Archbishop of Canterbury – a hard man and a hard-line Anglican – conducted a purge of the University's principal officers, denouncing them as Puritan heretics, little better than the wicked and despised Roman Catholics. Laud picked out Lawrence as a reliable supporter and appointed him as Proctor, a post of supervisory and disciplinary importance. In the short time he occupied it Lawrence performed his duties greatly to Laud's satisfaction, playing a full part in the purging of the Puritans.

In 1632 Lawrence further adorned his academic credentials by obtaining the degree of Bachelor of Divinity. However, this seemingly upright and undeniably very clever man of the cloth soon strayed by fathering a child, whom they named John, on a young lady called Amphilis Twigden, who was pregnant when he married her in 1633. The marriage deprived Lawrence of his College Fellowship, for which bachelor status was mandatory, and his resignation was inevitable. Thus we can say that if this Oxford academic and priest had not shared the amorous habits of many of the undergraduates he was intended to supervise, there might have been no American family of Washingtons and the first President of the USA would have been someone else . . .

Lawrence Washington's first church – All Saints at Purleigh, Essex

Lawrence, however, was able to rescue his career at least partially, for he soon obtained appointment as rector of the wealthy parish of Purleigh in Essex. The reasonably generous stipend must have come as something of a blessing to him as he had left Oxford in debt, owing 17 shillings and 10 pence personally and a sum of over £9 that he had kindly but unwisely guaranteed on behalf of a pupil. The Brasenose Bursar made a note to remind himself "Mr. Washington to be sued" but apparently the matter was overlooked. (In 1924 a group of American and Canadian academics were visiting Brasenose and, on learning that the personal debt remained unpaid, one of the Americans produced a pound note in settlement – and kindly invited the College to keep the change!)

Though Lawrence's indulgence in pre-marital sex was frowned on by the Church, it was not fatal to his reputation: for many a priest, both before and after him, demonstrated a similar proclivity. Were they all to have been de-frocked, the priesthood's numbers would have been more than a little diminished; thus a shrug of the Bishop's shoulders usually signalled the end of the matter! What is certain is that Lawrence solid Anglican religious views and his ability to put them across to others ensured his continuing favour. Quite possibly he was appointed to Purleigh on Archbishop Laud's own say-so, for the county of Essex was a hotbed of folk with Puritan leanings and had sent radical MPs to Parliament. In those circumstances, a capable and theologically-sound man who shared Laud's views was essential.

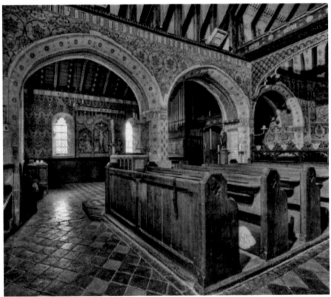

Interior of Lawrence Washington's second church,
at Little Braxted, Essex

However, Lawrence again became unstuck at the height of the English Civil War in 1643, when the religious climate moved radically against him and those who thought like him, for in that year the Puritans seized control of Parliament and sought revenge on their Anglican rivals. Lawrence was named as a "scandalous and malignant priest" and deprived of his benefice. For good measure the indictment added that he was "a common frequenter of alehouses, not only himself sitting daily tippling there but also encouraging others in that beastly vice and hath been oft drunk . . . and has published [announced] them to be traitors that lend [money] to or assist the Parliament". Of course, we do not know whether the allegation of inebriation was wholly true or not, for when you wish to bring a man down – particularly if you believe you are doing God's work – a little character assassination comes in very handy. Certainly, others who knew Lawrence testified to moderate drinking habits and at this distance we simply cannot know the strength of the allegations. Whatever the truth, expulsion from Purleigh was a severe blow to him but he did manage to secure a substitute living, albeit a very much poorer one, in the lesser parish of Braxted about five miles away, probably through the patronage and sympathy of the Lord of the Manor there.

After a decade of quieter service at Braxted, Lawrence's life came to an end in 1653 and he was buried at All Saint's Church at Maldon in Essex. The church now contains a 'Washington Window', presented in 1928 by the citizens of Malden, Massachusetts, which was founded by Joseph Hills of the English Maldon. (Spellings were flexible in those days.) Though he died with few worldly assets to pass on to his children, Lawrence unquestionably bequeathed them something more valuable: a pool of talented genes.

Lawrence and Amphilis's aforesaid son, John, emigrated to Virginia at about the time of his father's death. There he displayed a flair for enterprise and soon began to accumulate land and slaves, the latter not at that time something which disturbed the consciences of more than a few. Unquestionably, John's most important feat – and that of his fellow emigrants, brother Lawrence junior and sister Margaret – was to continue the family line on the far side of the Atlantic. On February 22nd 1732 (in other words, about fifty years after John's arrival in the New World) John's direct descendant Augustine Washington and his wife Mary welcomed into existence the one-day-to-be-famous George. Augustine's forte was tobacco planting (for which, of course, slaves in abundance were needed). Thus George Washington was born into a prosperous family of Virginian planters and consequently enjoyed the benefit of a pleasant childhood, spent mainly at Ferry Farm in Stafford County near Fredericksburg (named in honour of Frederick, Prince of Wales).

It had been intended originally that George Washington should cross the Atlantic to attend Appleby Grammar School in Cumbria in England, just as his two elder brothers and, before them, his father Augustine had done. But Augustine's death when George was only eleven apparently decided his widowed mother to keep him at home with her for company. At about 15, George expressed an interest in joining the Royal Navy but once again his mother had reservations, this time about the hardships and dangers of a seafaring life, and he was persuaded instead to qualify for the mundane but safe profession of land surveyor. For this purpose he attended William and Mary College at Williamsburg (named in honour of King William III and his wife). After qualifying, and thanks to the Washington family's friendship with Lord Fairfax of Cameron – born at exquisite Leeds Castle in Kent in England but by then resident on the vast estates his family also owned in Virginia – the young Washington was appointed to the well-paid post of Surveyor of Culpeper County. Soon he was to make the first of what were to be many land acquisitions on his own behalf. His military connections stem from this time, too, for on the death of his elder brother (yet another Lawrence) who had been Adjutant General of the Virginia Militia, George was himself appointed as a militia Major. He certainly looked the part, for he was a man of soldierly bearing, six feet tall and of commanding appearance. Following these beginnings, his subsequent military and political careers can broadly be divided into four phases.

The first phase comprised the abandonment of surveying for seven years of more or less full-time fighting, in various capacities, in victorious alliance with British forces from the mother country against the French and Indians, during which period he rose to the command of the Virginia Regiment. Despite the many daily demands on his time, he was able to keep comprehensive journals and make copies of his many letters, from which we are able to glean multitudes about his views and experiences. On examining these writings, one is struck by how repeatedly and ardently Washington emphasises his Englishness, his loyalty to the Crown and his detestation of the French. ("We know the character of the traitorous French.") On the outbreak of war against the French, Washington addressed his men as follows:

"You see, gentlemen soldiers, that it hath pleased our most gracious sovereign to declare war against the French King, and (for diverse good causes but more particularly for their ambitious encroachments on his American dominions) to pronounce all the said French King's subjects and vassals to be enemies to his crown and dignity . . . and though our utmost endeavours can contribute but little to the advancement of his Majesty's honour and the interest of his governments, yet let us show our willing obedience to the best of kings, and by a strict attachment to his royal commands, demonstrate the love and loyalty we bear to his sacred person . . . " How Washington's views were to change!

Moreover, he considered that his fellow citizens were sometimes too content to rely on the British forces from the mother country to defend them and "the possessions of his Majesty against the attempts and hostilities of the French" and urged that they "should rouse from the lethargy we have fallen into, [and display] the heroic spirit of every free-born Englishman to attest the rights and privileges of our king . . . and rescue from the invasions of a usurping enemy our Majesty's property, his dignity and land". On another occasion, after being congratulated by the Virginia House of Burgesses on leading a successful action by his Virginia Regiment, Washington replied: "[We] cannot help testifying our grateful acknowledgements for your high sense of what we shall always esteem a Duty to our Country and the best of Kings". This "best of Kings" was King George II – how far was his son, King George III, to fall from Washington's grace!

Washington certainly enjoyed battle personally: "I heard the bullets whistle, and, believe me, there is something charming in the sound". And whilst honing the military skills he allied to his personal bravery, he derived much benefit from studying the Native Americans' hit-and-run tactics and their clever use of cover, which contrasted with the more formal set-piece engagements which mostly characterised European warfare. Even early on, when serving alongside British General Braddock, he warned that General about the need to adapt to North American conditions, a warning which Braddock ignored and which led to that officer's bad defeat at 'Red Indian' hands.

Another recurrent theme of Washington's letters and journals during this period of fighting the French and Indians is his frequently-expressed dissatisfaction with the performance of the Virginian troops under his command. There are repeated references to wide-scale desertion, drunkenness and slackness in obeying orders. He wrote to a subordinate (on one of many similar occasions): "I have sent you one of the Mutiny Bills which you are . . . to frequently read to them. Further, acquaint them that if any soldier deserts, although he return himself, he shall be hanged". The threat of hanging was not made idly, as shown on not a few subsequent occasions. For example he wrote of several men under sentence of death: "The first for his cowardice at the action at Edwards's; the others for desertion. I have a warrant from the Governor for shooting Lewis, and shall delay the execution until the arrival of the new recruits. [Washington was obviously determined to teach the new men an unforgettable lesson right at the start.] The others were tried but today and the proceedings of the Court will be sent to the Governor. If he approves the sentences, I shall make it my particular care to see them executed too, as I shall every individual that offends in like cases". (At this point, it is very difficult to discern the nascent ability of the colonists' forces to successfully take on, as of course they later did, the regular forces of the British Crown.)

But despite his loyalty to the King and despite his fighting as a comrade-in-arms of troops born in the motherland, we can discern at this time the earliest stirrings of Washington's ultimate dissatisfaction with royal rule. Three things in particular rankled. The first was the stipulation that no American-born officer, however senior and experienced, could give direct orders to a British officer, however junior and 'raw'; second, that American-born officers could not qualify for a full King's commission, which was plainly militarily ridiculous; and third, the fact that American-born officers, doing the same job and facing the same enemy as 'home-grown' officers from the British Isles, enjoyed – if that is the word – far inferior pay and conditions. This was plainly unfair and Washington regularly protested about it. He wrote to the Governor of Virginia: "I really believe . . . we should be treated as gentlemen and officers and not have [to tolerate] the most trifling pay that ever was given to English officers". On another occasion, he wrote "that our complaints are not frivolous but founded upon strict reason", adding that he was not personally acquisitive except for obtaining "honour by serving faithfully my King and Country". Returning to the theme yet again at a later date, he wrote "we are greatly inferior in respect of profitable advantages, yet we have the same spirit to serve our Gracious King as [Regular Army officers] have and are as ready and willing to sacrifice our lives for our Country as them . . . This will be a cancer that will grate on some officers of this Regiment [the Virginia Regiment] beyond all measure, to serve upon such different terms when their Lives, their Fortunes and their Characters are equally and, I dare say, as effectually exposed as those happy enough to have King's Commissions".

Surely we can detect, in this single yet telling example, the frequent insensitivity of the motherland's ruling classes to their kith and kin in the burgeoning colonies, an insensitivity which, perhaps more than any specific issue (even taxation), gave rise to the ultimate struggle for independence.

The second of the four phases of Washington's life began when the French and their 'Red Indian' allies were finally defeated in 1759. From then until 1774, the militarily highly-experienced Washington lived the life of a prosperous aristocrat at the Washington family estate at Mount Vernon. He acquired a wife, Martha Custis, a wealthy widow who brought into the marriage yet more land and made him a rich man indeed. He enjoyed an aristocratic lifestyle largely indistinguishable from the British upper classes across the Atlantic, favouring fox-hunting as a leisure pursuit and diversifying that passion with dances, card-playing, backgammon and billiards. In common with other Virginia planters he imported luxuries and other goods from England, paying for them principally by exporting his tobacco crop. For this, of course, he relied heavily on slaves. And to escape even minor restrictions legislation placed on the exploitation of slaves held for more than 12 months, on one day each year this crafty and (it must be said) ruthless member of high society dodged the law by decanting his slaves a few yards across the state border for just 24-hours and then immediately re-importing them.

Himself at the apex of the Virginian social scene, Washington admitted that he generally preferred "people of rank". As for the lower orders, he advised "treat them civilly . . . but keep them at a proper distance, for they will grow upon familiarity in proportion as you sink in authority". It is difficult indeed to distinguish in his views and lifestyle anything to separate him – this self-avowed Englishman – from the conservative British elite with whom he was shortly to mightily clash; certainly, no instinctive belief in democracy and the rule of the common man is apparent in anything he said or did. As in the case of Cromwell when he overthrew King Charles I in the previous century, he was rather more interested in promoting the rule of his own class and kind rather than furthering the ambitions of 'levellers'.

In 1758 at the age of thirty-seven Washington became a member of the Virginia Assembly and in his doings as an Assemblyman, we can discern the development of another crucial strand of his thought and of Colonial thinking generally: the subject of taxation. Following the successful conclusion of the French war, by means of the Stamp Act of 1765 the British Government sought to recoup from the flourishing colonists some of the great expenditure it had incurred in their defence, and indeed was still incurring in maintaining the large Redcoat garrison. The Act imposed a levy on every piece of paper used by the colonists, including newspapers, magazines, legal documents and playing cards. Many of the colonists, Washington by now amongst them, took the view that they had already contributed enough in blood and treasure to the costs of the war and that, in a time of peace, a garrison from the motherland was no longer required. The colonists were violently encouraged in their views by American newspapers which, as heavy consumers of newsprint, were naturally at the very forefront of protests. (The British Government must surely have wished it had had the wit to exempt them!) Riots ensued and the Act was repealed within a year. But further unpopular measures – most notably what the colonists called "the Intolerable Acts" of 1774 – were described by Washington as "an Invasion of our Rights and Privileges" and he called for a boycott of British goods. He told a friend: "I think the Parliament of Great Britain has no more right to put their hands in my pocket without my consent than I have to put my hands into yours for money". He expressed the opinion that the colonists must not submit to "acts of tyranny till custom and use shall make us tame and abject slaves, as the blacks we rule over with such arbitrary sway".

Of course, as a rich man Washington was no keener on taxes than anyone else, in America or in Britain, a view shared with greater justification by the poor of both territories! It must be recorded, however, that viewed objectively the level of British-imposed taxation in America was in itself of little more than minor financial consequence. In the classic American revolutionary phrase, it was the *principle* of "taxation without representation" that rankled more than anything else. If we look behind this, we can surely detect the true underlying cause of the American Revolution: a child is dependent on its parents but as it goes through its teenage years and enters adulthood, it becomes increasingly motivated to lead a life of its own, flexing its own muscles, following its own path, fulfilling its own destiny. If we consider Britain as the parent and Colonial America as the child, we are driven to conclude that the British 'establishment' failed to recognise the analogy and attempted to tie the colonists too closely to its apron strings. Had Britain adopted a more relaxed attitude, as it did in the case of Canada, Australia and New Zealand, things might have been very different. (On the outbreak of World War in August 1914, their loyalty was such that all three of these nations promised the British Government, "We are with you to the last man and the last shilling".) But the British did what they did, and Washington and his fellow colonists did what they did, and the result was shattering.

Thus we move to the third and pivotal phase of Washington's career: his leadership during the Revolution, both political and military. The outline of the story is well-known, ranging as it does from the nadir of his military fortunes at Valley Forge in the (for him) near-disastrous winter of 1777/78 to the decisive Franco-American defeat of the British at Yorktown in 1781, but three factors stand out. The first is his role as commander of the American Army (usually called the 'Continental Army') – from virtually the start to the finish of hostilities, and, in co-operation with Congress, his control of strategy. A man of admirable resilience, he fought undaunted through the darkest days to final victory. The second factor is the great emphasis he placed on military professionalism, exemplified by his appointment of the German General Baron von Steuben, a veteran of the Prussian General Staff, to train the rebel troops and impose discipline. (Steuben's influence went far to eliminate the kinds of deficiencies in the colonists' fighting forces which had driven Washington to near-despair in earlier life.) The third factor is Washington's use and encouragement of frontier riflemen, long-practised in hunting and in defending themselves against predators and marauding 'Red Indians'. These men were a formidable enemy when opposed to the traditional British musket and bayonet. Even so, Washington and his men lost the majority of the battles; their three main successes, at Boston in 1776, Saratoga in 1777 and Yorktown [5] in 1781, all came from trapping the British far from base with much larger numbers of troops. Finally, Washington had a great capacity to inspire people and embodied in himself the spirit of resistance to the Crown – the Crown he had once so revered. It was these things, together with his enormous powers of resilience which led to his ultimate success and generated the war-weariness to which the British finally succumbed after seven years far, far from home – not unlike the twentieth-century descendants of Washington's men in Vietnam. The other, and crucial, contribution to victory was, of course, the colonists' alliance with the French, the French whom until so recently Washington had reviled – the first example of the axiom of twentieth-century American Secretary of State Henry Kissinger:

---

5 For more about the Yorktown, please see the chapter
   The American Revolution and the Reluctant British General

"America has no permanent friends or enemies, only interests". We must add that this is true of almost every nation – indeed, Kissinger was only echoing a remark about Britain which had been made long before by Lord Palmerston.

In the course of the war, Washington had formed an intimacy with all the leading politicians of the putative nation and established himself in the public mind as a man of the highest talent. These were the things that were to set him up for the final phase of his public life. This began when he emerged from a period of post-war rest and recuperation at Mount Vernon. (Whilst there, it was impiously recorded, he had had the leisure to prepare and submit to Congress an invoice for $450,000 for compensation for expenses incurred during the eight-year conflict; it was cheekily said the invoice was "detailed as to small items, vague concerning large ones".) Fully renewed and restored in mind and body, in 1789 Washington was unanimously elected first President of the new United States of America at a Constitutional Convention of representatives of all the thirteen former colonies. (Until this point, each had continued to govern itself as a separate entity, for many Americans harboured severe reservations about the creation of a Union, fearing a Federal Government might replicate the control over their lives hitherto exercised by the British Parliament.) But Washington's wisdom, together with his unflappability in the face of political difficulties at home and abroad, succeeded in establishing the infant country on a firm foundation. Washington gave up the Presidency in 1797 but survived only two more years, dying at the age of 67.

Before closing this account, one event of Washington's presidency merits recording in a little more detail, for it represents one of history's most delicious ironies. It took the form of an insurrection against the Federal Government and in its cause and course it uncannily paralleled on a smaller scale the Revolutionary War fought by Washington himself against that very Government's British predecessor. Popularly known as the Whiskey Rebellion, it was triggered in 1791 when Washington and his Treasury Secretary, Alexander Hamilton, imposed a tax on all distilled spirits, the first to be levied on a domestic product. This was done as part of a programme to reduce the national debt incurred in fighting the Revolutionary War. (Stamp Act, French and Indian war debt, anybody?) Opposition was fierce and immediate, especially amongst the farmers of the western frontier regions, long accustomed to distilling their surplus grain and corn into whiskey. Riots, violence, killings and the intimidation of tax officials replicated exactly the earlier campaigns against the British. There were skirmishes and small battles. Even the intellectual justification for the disturbances was identical – the imposition of taxes by a central government without local representation. In Pittsburgh a gathering of 7,000 citizens even called for independence from the United States, for re-union with Britain and for emulating the French revolution by introducing the guillotine to eliminate the ruling elite! In 1794 Washington was forced to raise an army of 13,000 men to suppress the heartlands of the rebellion – and even that was not easy, for it triggered anti-draft riots. But, in the face of the Federal Government's determination, order was finally restored – though evading the whiskey tax long remained a national sport.

On this concluding note, if you are one of those who appreciates the virtues of Jack Daniels' or Jim Beam's bourbon or of Scotch whisky, you might care to raise a glass to the honour of George Washington, his ancestral home in Essex and to the producers of all heart-warming liquids, American and British alike!

ESSEX

The Captain of *The Mayflower*

As almost every schoolchild learns, the *Mayflower* was the vessel that carried the Pilgrim Fathers to the New World in 1620 and few ships are better known, for the men, women and children aboard her were to play an historic role in the British colonisation of America. The captain of the vessel was a seafarer from Harwich in Essex, by name one Christopher Jones. It is his story and the story of his ship that we tell here. (The epic exploits of the Pilgrim Fathers themselves are recounted in other chapters of this book.)

Jones was born in Harwich in 1570 or thereabouts, the son of Christopher Jones senior and his wife Sybil. The Jones' family home in Kings Head Street, in which young Christopher grew up, has survived 400 years of tumultuous English history. And standing opposite it still is the family home of young Christopher's first wife, Sara Twitt, nowadays a public house called *The Alma*. Christopher and Sybil's union was thus a classic case of a boy marrying the girl next door – or, pedantically, the girl just across the street. Their marriage ceremony took place in nearby St. Nicholas Church in December 1593 and the church, too, continues to grace the town, though it was largely re-built in 1822. However, tucked away in its northern aisle is the original Norman font, now nearly 1.000 years old, in which Christopher was baptised. (Another Christopher, Captain Christopher Newport, was also baptised in it. [6])

When Sara died in 1603, Christopher re-married, his bride on this occasion being a young widow of 21 called Josian Gray – and once more St. Nicholas Church was the venue. Josian's late husband had himself been a noted mariner, with friends amongst the captains who had fought against the Spanish Armada in its foiled attempt to

---

6   For further information about Captain Christopher Newport, see the chapter
     Otley Hall: The Birthplace of British America

invade Britain in 1588. Harwich had demonstrated its loyalty to Queen Elizabeth I (who called Harwich "a pretty town") by sending three ships to bolster the English fleet. Socially, as in the case of so many other towns at that time, many if not most inhabitants were firm believers in witchcraft and shortly after Christopher's second marriage a number of local women were hanged. Women labelled as harlots were much luckier, 'merely' being dragged through the streets behind a cart and given a good whipping.

Christopher Jones' home in Kings Head Street, Harwich

Christopher's father and grandfather were both Harwich skippers and he served his seafaring apprenticeship alongside them. The port itself taught him some valuable seafaring lessons, for it lay behind some dangerous sandbars frequently assailed by savage North Sea storms. (On one occasion, thirty ships were wrecked.) At age eighteen he inherited his first part-share in a ship and by his mid-thirties he was successful and prosperous enough to commission the construction of a vessel of his own, which he named *Josian* in honour of his wife.

*Now the Alma Inn, this was once the home
of Christopher Jones' first wife*

By 1609 Christopher had acquired quarter-ownership of "the *Mayflower* of Harwich", as she is called in a surviving document, probably having traded-in the *Josian* in what we would now call a 'part-exchange deal'. *Mayflower* was not only "of Harwich" but almost certainly built there as well. She has been described as follows: "A typical English merchant ship of the 17th century – square-rigged and beak-bowed, with high, castle-like structures fore and aft that served to protect the ship's crew and the main deck from the elements; but having on her stern the aforesaid 30-feet high, square aft-castle made her extremely difficult to sail against the wind. This awkward configuration particularly hampered her in sailing well against the North Atlantic's prevailing Westerlies." She was probably about 100 feet in length, 25 feet in breadth at her widest point, with about 12 feet of her hull laying below the waterline. She had three masts – mizzen (aft), main (midship) and foremast, together with a spritsail at the bow. She also had three primary levels – main deck, gun deck and cargo hold. Christopher Jones' cabin was on the main deck at the stern, and measured a less than palatial ten feet by seven feet. As in the case of many merchant ships of the time, she was fairly heavily armed to provide a measure of protection against the pirates and privateers all too likely to be encountered on many a European trade route. Her most formidable weapon was normally a bronze cannon called a 'minion', weighing half-a-ton and able to fire a 3 1/2lb cannonball for nearly a mile. She also had a 'saker' cannon of about a quarter-ton in weight and various smaller guns. Conditions for the crew (which ranged in size from thirty to fifty, depending on the nature of any particular voyage) and the passengers were primitive and crowded, and sanitary facilities were either a bucket or 'over the side'. Except in fair conditions and on relatively short voyages – perhaps done in stages around western European and Mediterranean coasts – a miserable passage was usually guaranteed and food and water were highly susceptible to deterioration on lengthy trips without interim ports of call.

In about 1611 Christopher transferred the home port of the vessel from Harwich to Rotherhithe on the Thames, a mile downstream from the Tower of London, and acquired a house there for himself and his family. His motive was to take advantage of the expanding maritime trade from and to the nation's capital city. Especially profitable was the wine trade, consumption increasing in step with the burgeoning wealth of the landowning classes. On his last trip before carrying the Pilgrims, Jones brought back fifty tons of wine from Spain. By this time *Mayflower* was an ageing ship nearing the end of the usual working life of about fifteen years for an English merchant vessel of that era but the canny and experienced Jones partly compensated for the age of the vessel by recruiting experienced seamen to help him on the forthcoming American voyage, including two Master's Mates with previous voyages to the New World already 'under their belt'. *Mayflower* embarked her first group of about sixty-five Puritan passengers in London in mid-July and made her way to Southampton, where she rendezvoused with the *Speedwell*, a leaky 60-ton pinnace which had brought the Leyden contingent of about 31 men, women and children from Holland. (These were English Puritans who had been living there for several years in its more tolerant religious climate.) As in the case of the *Mayflower*, *Speedwell* was not a young ship, having been launched in 1577; amongst other challenges to her strength, she had fought against the Spanish Armada in 1588. *Mayflower* and *Speedwell*, after repairs had been made to the latter to repair leaks, set off together from Southampton for the New World on 29th July 1620. But *Speedwell* proved a problem by still taking on water, and both ships had to put into Dartmouth for further remedial work to the smaller vessel. Optimistically, they set off once more but about 300 miles from Land's End in Cornwall they were forced to turn about and come back to Plymouth, *Speedwell* again the culprit. Unsurprisingly, the decision was taken to abandon her and to continue with the *Mayflower* alone, though this of course involved a reduction in passenger-carrying capacity. In consequence, eleven of the Leyden contingent transferred to the larger ship, increasing the crowding; twenty returned to London where they tarried for several months until securing passages on another vessel and re-uniting with their co-religionists on the far side of the Atlantic.

Mayflower, 102 passengers aboard, finally departed on 16th September, the delays meaning that she left just as the autumn Atlantic gales were starting. The voyage took a dreadful 66 days, *Mayflower* fighting the gales most of the way and sustaining ruptures in her planking. William Bradford, the de facto leader of the Pilgrim party, kept a log of the voyage, which reveals just how tough it was. For instance, he wrote of himself and his companions: "After they enjoyed fair winds and weather, they encountered, many times, crosswinds, and many fierce storms, with which the ship was thoroughly shaken and her upperworks made very leaky; and one of the main beams amidships was downed and cracked, which put them in some fear that the ship could not perform the voyage. So some of the chiefs of the company, perceiving the mariners to fear the condition of the ship, as appeared by their mutterings, they entered into serious consultation with the master and other officers of the ship, to consider whether to return, rather than to cast themselves into desperate and inevitable peril. And truly there was great distraction and difference of opinion amongst the mariners themselves. But in examining of all opinions, the master and others affirmed they knew the ship to be strong and firm underwater." We can confidently read into this that all of Christopher Jones's leadership and morale-preserving skills had to be brought into play to steady the nerves of the apprehensive landlubbers, not to mention more than a few members of his crew. The resourceful and ingenious Jones and his men certainly rose to the challenge of keeping the ship seaworthy, for they improvised a solid repair to the buckled main beam by using a great iron screw to raise it back into place. They also succeeded as in re-caulking the seams, a hugely creditable achievement whilst in the midst of an unfriendly ocean.

A modern replica of the Mayflower

Bradford continued: "They committed themselves to the will of God and resolved to proceed [despite the damage]. In many of the [continuing] storms the winds were so fierce, and the seas so high, they could not bear a knot of sail but were forced to heave to for many days together." On one occasion, in a "mighty storm a strapping young man called John Howland was, with a lurch of the ship, thrown into the sea; but it pleased God that he caught hold of the ropes which hung overboard. [God seeming, however, not to have been sufficiently pleased to prevent him from being flung into the ocean in the first place!] "He held his hold (though he was many feet under water) till he was hauled up by the same rope to the brim of the water, and then with a boathook and other means got into the ship again and his life saved."

In a classic understatement, Bradford records that when finally "they fell with that land which is called Cape Cod they were not a little joyful"! The Pilgrims selected what is now Plymouth Harbour as their anchorage and settlement. Jones and his crew remained there for several months while they recovered as well as they could from the strains of the voyage and the illnesses it had brought on. They put back to sea, bound for England, on 5th April 1621 and arrived back at Rotherhithe a month later, the return voyage taking less than half the time of the outward leg. Jones enjoyed for a while a re-union with his family, friends and native country, but in the summer he resumed his trading voyages to mainland Europe. Sadly, the Pilgrim voyage had undermined his health to an irretrievable extent and in March 1622, at the age of 52, he died. He was buried in St. Mary's Church at Rotherhithe, never to know the ultimate success of the passengers he had carried but today renowned as an intrepid Essex man who made an indelible mark on history.

What of the fate of *Mayflower* herself? She was inspected by Jones's probate lawyers who, unsurprisingly, found her aged and tired. They concluded she could be sold only for scrap, in effect for the value of her re-usable timber, and she was disposed of for £50. Five anchors were sold, too, for £25. Together with some of her weapons and equipment, a total of £128 was raised.

The timbers of the Mayflower, Mayflower Barn, Jordans

Intriguingly, in the 1920s the antiquarian J. Rendell Harris established that in 1624 the *Mayflower*'s timbers had been sold to Thomas Russell, landowner and farmer, of Old Jordans on the edge of the Chiltern Hills in South Buckinghamshire, and that Russell used them to construct a large barn. Known today as The Mayflower Barn, it stands to this day and is a thing not only of history but of beauty, too. Thus, relics of *Mayflower*, though now firmly ashore, metaphorically continue to sail boldly on, perhaps still under the ghostly direction of her master, the famous Essex Captain Christopher Jones.

ESSEX

The Family Who Gave the World the Flying Machine

It was in or about 1485 that the multi-facetted Italian genius Leonardo da Vinci described his unprecedented proposals for flying machines, his incredibly fertile mind conceiving not only of powered aeroplanes but helicopters too. As one might imagine of the man who painted perhaps the most famous portrait of all time, the *Mona Lisa,* he illustrated these concepts with drawings worthy of his allied reputation as one of the world's finest-ever artists.

It was rather more than one hundred years after Leonardo achieved these imaginative leaps (in 1606 to be precise), that there was born in England at Wrightsbridge in Essex a man called Samuel Wright who was never to see anything but birds take to the skies, nor to imagine that anything other than birds could possibly do so. But it was two descendants of this Essex man who were ultimately to make a reality of Leonardo's dream by achieving the world's first mechanically-powered flight. Those two descendants are now known to history as the Wright Brothers.

Their English ancestor, the aforesaid Samuel, was a member of the Wright family headed by wealthy Sir John Wright of Dagenham (later Kelvedon) Hall. As a young man, Samuel Wright attended Puritan-leaning Emmanuel College at Cambridge University. He was very much at his theological ease there, for he was himself a convinced Puritan – in other words, one of those who believed that the Church of England was still besmirched, as they saw it, by wicked Roman Catholic beliefs and practices. In 1625 he married an equally devout Puritan, Margaret Dickerson, and over the next few years Margaret gave birth to four children. However, the couples' religious beliefs were so uncomfortably at odds with those of

*The ancient Cross Keys Inn at Dagenham,
which dates back to the 1400s and would have been
familiar to the Wright Brothers' ancestors*

mainstream society that they eventually felt compelled to leave their English homeland. Thus in 1633 they took ship aboard the *Arbella* (which had previously carried John Winthrop and his adherents) and joined the many other English Puritans already dwelling in the New World. By 1636 or thereabouts they were settled in Springfield, Massachusetts, taking up residence on what is now Main Street, a stone's throw from the historic First Church. Samuel went on to achieve a modest prosperity by buying a share in the profits of a toll bridge and himself built a mill. He was also appointed Deacon of the First Congregational Church, for which he was paid fifty shillings a month. The Wrights continued to prosper in the generations after Samuel's death in 1665 and by the 1800s a branch of the family was flourishing in the frontier town of Dayton, Ohio. The Wrights' links with religion had survived the passage of time and the head of family in Dayton was a Bishop, one Milton Wright.

In 1878 Milton performed a small act of kindness by buying his young sons Orville and Wilbur a toy helicopter based on a design by the French aeronautical pioneer, Alphonse Penaud. It was about a foot long and made of paper, bamboo and cork and had a rubber-band powered rotor. The brothers played with it constantly and ascribed to Penaud's helicopter their lifelong fascination with flight. However, for a variety of reasons, the brothers' formal education was skimpy and after dabbling in the newspaper and printing business, to make a living they opened a bicycle sales and repair shop to capitalise on the new craze for cycling. Before long, they were designing and manufacturing their own two-wheelers.

However, none of this distracted them from their obsession with the skies and they followed with intense interest the progress of flying machines of various kinds designed by the German Otto Lilienthal, the Englishman Sir George Cayley, the Frenchman Clement Ader, the American Samuel Langley and others. By 1900 the brothers were flying gliders of their own design and construction at Kitty Hawk, North Carolina. But they grew in the conviction – as did others – that mastery of the skies could be truly achieved only by mechanically-powered machines. Consequently, they set about building a petrol-engined biplane (i.e. with two wings, one above the other). This came to be known to history as the 'Wright Flyer 1', and on 17th December 1903 it made three successful flights, of 120 feet, 175 feet and 200 feet respectively. It was Orville who piloted the Flyer on its initial 12-second hop and who, therefore, laid claim to piloting the world's first successful flight by a powered and manned heavier-than-air machine. Orville's Essex ancestors would surely have been stunned by such a miracle.

Over time the brothers went on to develop improved and much superior models. Their designs were distinguished by their great manoeurability, for Orville and Wilbur perceived the importance of controlling what aeronautical engineers call roll, pitch and yaw, and ultimately they succeeded in incorporating mechanisms which enabled all these to be directed by the pilot. In 1905 in the Wright Flyer 3 they achieved a flight of an unprecedented 39 minutes and there can be little doubt that they produced the most successful of all early flying machines.

An early Wright Brothers' flight. The launching rail can be clearly seen and wind-assistance was required.

However, it is incumbent on us to record that the Wright brothers' widely-accepted claim to be the *first* people to successfully fly a piloted heavier-than-air machine does not go unchallenged. Aviation's controlling body, the Federation Aeronautique International (the FAI), laid down a number of criteria by which such a feat could be judged, amongst them that the flight should be accomplished in *calm weather* and with the aircraft able to take off by *its own means*. In fact, the Wright Flyer 1 was able to get into the air *only* with the assistance of a launch rail *and* a strong wind. (Later, the brothers used a launching catapault.) Thus, by official FAI criteria – and, it seems to many, by the criteria of common sense – Orville and Wilbur's first flight or flights did not and do not qualify.

Contending for the official distinction is, principally, the Brazilian Alberto Santos-Dumont who met all the full criteria in an officially-observed flight in France in 1906, in still-air conditions using an aircraft of his own design and fitted with its own wheeled undercarriage. (There are other claimants, too, which the interested reader can no doubt research for him- or herself. It must also be added, curiously, that it was not until Santos-Dumont's success that the Wright Brothers laid public claim to their efforts in 1903, which gave rise to suspicion in some minds.)

But the fact remains, the Wright Brothers were geniuses of the skies and within a few years' had developed craft which were clearly the best of all early flying machines, even if not truly the *first*. Consequently, they will ever be remembered for their massive contribution to the progress of aviation and the science of aerodynamics. Few, though, now recall that the genes which harboured Orville and Wilbur's inventiveness stem from a family which dwelt long ago in the English county of Essex.

ESSEX

Baseball, the great *British* Game!

The English county of Essex is nowadays home to five modern Baseball teams, a larger number than any other county in Britain. Nationally, however, Baseball is an almost-invisible minority sport, for its British adherents are swamped by the vastly greater number of Soccer and Cricket addicts. To many people this will come as no surprise because, of course, "baseball is *the* quintessentially American game". Isn't it?

Well, the only accurate answer to that is a resounding "no", for baseball is in all its fundamentals the centuries-old English game of Rounders. Since its migration to Colonial America, rounders has simply undergone a little transatlantic tinkering so as to form its modern American cousin. Rounders has been played by generation after generation of folk in England – mainly youngsters – though in recent times its popularity has suffered a marked decline. However, the fact that the one game is the offspring of the other remains instantly and indisputably recognisable. Even the very word "baseball" itself was used by the English as an alternative name for their sport hundreds of years ago. (Naturally, there are nowadays differences of *detail* between the two games in light of their separate development over time and an ocean apart, but they are relatively minor.)

Consider the following definitions:

'Rounders' is defined by its British governing body as *a striking and fielding game that involves hitting a small, hard, leather-cased ball with a rounded-end bat. The players score by running around the four bases on the field. There are a number of innings at which teams alternate at batting and fielding. A maximum of nine players are allowed at any time. Points are scored by the batting team when one of their players completes a circuit past four bases without being 'out'.*

'Baseball' in the USA is defined by an expert American source *as a bat and ball game played between two teams who take turns batting and fielding. The batting team attempts to score runs by hitting a ball with a rounded bat then running around a series of four bases. The fielding team tries to prevent runs by getting hitters out. A run is scored when a player advances round the bases and returns to home plate.*

In will be seen immediately that the two definitions could be transposed and still retain perfect accuracy. Notwithstanding this, your writer knows that in common with fellow sports fans world-wide, American baseball enthusiasts are patriotically inclined and most do not take easily to the fact (of which many are not even aware) that their game is fundamentally un-American! Your writer therefore accepts he is likely to receive intensive verbal castigation from across the Atlantic (a fancy, high-falutin' English way of saying he expects to get his ears boxed!) Nevertheless, he's started so he'll finish . . .

Rounders itself probably has its origins in even older games, including Stoolball, Trapball, Tutball, and Dog and Cat. The earliest known mention of stoolball is in a poem written in 1330 by Englishman William Pagula, who felt strongly that the game ought not to be played in churchyards. Trapball, too, was played in 14th century England and components of these traditional pastimes ultimately evolved into rounders. By 1672 rounders was also known by the alternative name of baseball, for in that year the English churchman Bishop Thomas Wilson wrote of his intense dislike of those who indulged in 'Morris-dancing, cudgel-playing, baseball and cricket' on Sundays. The first mention of baseball in printed book form was to come a little later when in 1744 the English publisher John Newbery produced *A Little Pretty Pocket Book* for children. He encapsulated baseball in the following rhyme:

Base-ball

The Ball once struck off,
Away flies the Boy
To the next destin'd Post
And then home with Joy.

Newbery went on to draw an analogy between baseball and the pleasure of a home run and the triumph of British adventurers in exploring far-off lands and returning to their native country with valuable goods and treasure:

Thus Britons for Lucre
Fly over the Main;
But with Pleasure transported,
Return back again.

In 1748 no less a personage than Frederick, Prince of Wales, the father of King George III, is recorded as playing a baseball game in London. The Prince was most probably an enthusiast, for the following year he and his team are reported as playing against a side captained by Lord Middlesex; the level of the teams' commitment must have been high, for the *Whitehall Post* advised its readers that "notwithstanding the Weather was extreme bad, they continued playing several hours".

In 1755 a book called *The Card* written by the English clergyman John Kidgell mentions that "the younger part of [our] family . . . retired to an interrupted party at baseball . . . " By 1768 an entry for baseball appeared in *A General Dictionary of the English Language* and before the end of the century a German book on popular pastimes described 'Englische Baseball' in detail over seven pages e.g. "the batter has three attempts to hit the ball while at the home plate". Thirty years later, in 1798-99, Jane Austen wrote Northanger Abbey, in it describing her heroine Catherine Morland as preferring "cricket, baseball, riding on horseback and running about the country to books". This feminine aspect of love of the game was emphasised in the 1820s by another English author, Mary Russell Mitford, in this charming vignette from her *Village Sketch*: "Then comes a sun-burnt gipsy of six, beginning to grow tall and thin and to find the cares of the world gathering about her; with a pitcher [a water container] in one hand, a mop in the other, an old straw bonnet of ambiguous shape, half hiding her tangled hair; a tattered stuff petticoat, once green, hanging below an equally tattered cotton frock, once purple; her longing eyes fixed on a game of baseball at the corner of the green till she reaches the cottage door, flings down the mop and pitcher and darts off to her companions quite regardless of the storm of scolding with which her mother follows her runaway steps".

The first known American written references to baseball are not until 1786 when a Princeton student recorded in his diary: "A fine day, play baseball in the campus but am beaten for I miss both catching and striking the ball"; and in 1791, when a bylaw of the town of Pittsfield, Massachusetts banned "any game of wicket, cricket, baseball, batball, football, cats, fives, or any other game played with a ball" within eighty yards of the town meeting house to prevent damage to its windows. (Every game mentioned, it will be noted, was English.)

By the late 1800s, baseball in America was enjoying not only increasing popularity but growing financial success through the creation of semi-professional and professional teams. However, many patriotic Americans of the chest-beating variety (who exist in every nation, not excluding Britain) were unhappy that what was emerging as their national game was not merely *foreign* in origin but, even worse, an invention of their former British colonial masters. Their leader was Albert G. Spalding, head of the famous sporting goods company. He deemed it his patriotic duty to prove by hook-or-by-crook that baseball was American in *every* sense, even in origin. He therefore set up a hand-picked commission of inquiry – a commission of inquiry approximately as fair as the judges in a show trial under Josef Stalin. The Chairman, for example, was Abraham G. Mills, who had earlier declared at a banquet for 300 baseball enthusiasts in New York that he "wanted it distinctly understood patriotism and research" had established that the game of baseball was American in origin. His audience greeted this pronouncement with enthusiastic cries of "No rounders!" – thus effectively admitting the very reality they were loth to acknowledge! (The full story can be read in the excellent *Baseball: The Early Years* by American authors Harold and Dorothy Seymour, from which this quotation is taken). Unsurprisingly, the Spalding/Mills inquiry's finding was that (contrary to everything known hitherto) baseball had been invented at Cooperstown, New York in 1839 by General Abner Doubleday. One can only repeat the words of the present-day Official Historian of Major League Baseball, John Thorn, who has written: "This would have come as a surprise to Doubleday. But fifteen years after his death, he was annointed as the father of the game".

Through dint of repetition, money and influence, the propaganda spouted by Spalding and his successors proved so successful that its fictitious home of Cooperstown even became the location for The Baseball Hall of Fame. A brilliant and persistent combination of lies and half-truths did their job marvellously, and today millions of American baseball fans innocently yet fervently believe the opposite of the truth.

Meanwhile, back on the British side of the Atlantic, that cluster of five teams in Essex referred to by your writer at the start – and the handful of teams scattered elsewhere in the UK – continue to adore their Baseball . . . or should that be 'Rounders'?

LINCOLNSHIRE & NORFOLK

Pocahontas: She Saved an English Colonist & Conquered his Country with Love

A little before Christmas 1607 a man with the quintessentially English name of John Smith feared that his life was moments away from a brutal ending. He was 3,000 miles away from Lincolnshire, England, where his home village of Great Carlton nestled then, as it does today, amongst the delightful hills known as the Lincolnshire Wolds. It was but a few months earlier that he had departed from London as one of 104 pioneers aboard a little fleet of three ships bound for the New World, all intent on establishing a new British settlement to be named Jamestown in honour of King James I of England and VI of Scotland. Now, on the north shore of Virginia's York River, he was the captive of a tribe of Native Americans, having suffered the misfortune of falling into the hands of one of their hunting parties after having left the comparative safety of Jamestown to forage for food, of which the settlers were desperately short.

At first, Smith had some grounds for optimism about his fate, for he was initially promised he would be set free within a few days. But when marched before Powhatan, the 'king' or 'emperor' of the region's tribes, Smith's optimism evaporated. Writing of himself in the third person, he recorded that "at his [Smith's] entrance before the King, all the people gave a great shout . . . [a] long consultation was held but the conclusion was, two great stones were brought before Powhatan: then as many as could laid hands on him [Smith], dragged him to them and thereon laid his head, and being ready with their clubs, to beat out his brains. Pocahontas the King's dearest daughter, when no entreaty would prevail, got his head in her arms and laid her own upon his to save him from death." Much affected by his daughter's plea, to the dramatic extent of throwing herself between Smith and the warriors eager to inflict the fatal clubbing, Powhatan spared Smith's life and granted him freedom. The story is now a famous one in American history, depicted (with a little artistic licence) in stone on a frieze in the Capitol in Washington D.C.

Pocahontas saving John Smith: the frieze in the Capitol

Later, the saga of Smith and Pocahontas caught the imagination of the great English writer and poet, William Makepeace Thackeray, though as will be seen from the following stirring extract from his poem, he granted himself still greater licence to depart from the facts! But he does capture marvellously the essence of the dreadful scene, the fear that Smith must have felt, and the impulsive humanity of the Red Indian maid:

> *Wearied arm and broken sword*
> *Wage in vain the desperate fight:*
> *Round him press a countless horde,*
> *He is but a single knight.*
> *Hark! A cry of triumph shrill*
> *Through the wilderness resounds,*
> *As, with twenty bleeding wounds,*
> *Sinks the warrior, fighting still.*

Now they heap the fatal pyre,
And the torch of death they light:
Ah! 'tis hard to die of fire!
Who will shield the captive knight?
Round the stake with fiendish cry
Wheel and dance the savage crowd,
Cold the victim's mien, and proud,
And his breast is bared to die.

Who will shield the fearless heart?
Who avert the murderous blade?
From the throng, with sudden start,
See there springs an Indian maid.
Quick she stands before the knight,
'Loose the chain, unbind the ring,
I am the daughter of the king,
And I claim the Indian right!'

Dauntlessly she flings aside
Lifted axe and thirsty knife;
Fondly to his heart she clings,
And her bosom guards his life!
In the woods of Powhatan,
Still 'tis told by Indian fires,
How a daughter of their sires
Saved a captive Englishman.

One might think that Pocahontas had by this single deed contributed enough to the romance of history but no, more great drama was to come. Jamestown's relationships with the Native American tribes continued, sometimes peacefully, sometimes not, and thus it came about during an outbreak of hostilities in 1613 that in a reversal of fortune the English captured Pocahontas and held her for ransom – the meanest of acts, one might feel, in light of her having earlier saved an English life. Be that as it may, the English must have been drawn to her and she to them, for during her captivity she converted to Christianity and adopted the name Rebecca (though it is her original name that has gone down in history, and it is good that that should be so). Thankfully, the English eventually relented, thoughts of ransoming her were abandoned and she was given the freedom to return to her tribe and family. But she opted instead to remain with the English, not as a captive but as a free woman. Moreover, love of a particular Englishman was soon to fill the air for in April 1614 she married John Rolfe of Heacham Manor in Norfolk, who had arrived in Jamestown two years after John Smith and was to become the first Englishman to successfully cultivate Virginia tobacco. A son, Thomas, was born in January the following year. The marriage of the pair seems to have ushered in a considerable period of amicability between the English and the native tribes. Not only did Powhatan himself grant the newly-weds thousands of acres of land but, as one colonist wrote, "Since the wedding we have had friendly commerce and trade not only with Powhatan but also with his subjects round about us".

In 1616 John and Pocahontas and their little boy set sail for England for a prolonged visit. On arrival, she conquered the country with her charm and her loving disposition. Everywhere she went she was the subject of fascination and accorded the status of a Princess; she, in turn, was much amazed by the sights of the Old World – which, paradoxically, must have seemed a stunningly modern New World to her. The Bishop of London, to mention but one admirer, was delighted to play host to her. A fellow churchman who was present recorded: "Doctor King entertained her with festival state and pompe, beyond what I have seene in his hospitalitie offered to other Ladies. She carried herself as the Daughter of a King and was accordingly respected by persons of Honor." On Twelfth Night 1617 she attended a performance of Ben Jonson's masque *A Vision of Delight* at the Banqueting House, Whitehall. There she was "received by the King and graciously used".

The three Rolfes made a home in Brentford in Middlesex, and later John took Pocahontas and son John for a lengthy visit to his ancestral residence, the aforementioned Heacham Manor. Heacham village was a small place in those days – and not large now – and Norfolk was an isolated and distinctly non-cosmopolitan part of the country. Unsurprisingly, Pocahontas was a sensation there, a truly exotic figure. Generations later she is still remembered and her image is enshrined not merely in the Capitol in Washington D.C. but – surely an equal honour! – on the Heacham village sign. (Whilst staying at the Manor, Pocahontas is reputed to have planted the ancient mulberry tree which still stands in the grounds.)

Heacham Manor(now a hotel), visited by Pocahontas

Sadly, the story of Pocahontas was to end tragically, for a little before the Rolfe family's scheduled return to Virginia in April 1617, she died at the devastatingly early age of twenty-two. The cause was probably tuberculosis to which, as a non-European without previous exposure to it, she would have had little resistance. She was buried in the chancel of St. George's Church in Gravesend. She is commemorated there by a fine statue, as she is in Jamestown, Virginia itself. Husband John, widower that he now was, nevertheless carried out his intention of returning to Jamestown but survived there only five years, being killed in a Native American attack on his plantation in 1622. (Few things last, least of all peace between human beings.)

However, son John Rolfe junior, the product of the epic love between the Englishman and the 'Red Indian' princess, remained in Britain, placed in the care of his father's relatives. He was to receive a good education, marry and have children of his own. Thus the blood of Pocahontas flows in English veins to this day. The traditional name 'John Rolfe' has carried on down through the years, too, and recently its current proud bearer, 21st century John Rolfe, attended the celebrations to mark the 400th anniversary of Pocahontas's death.

LINCOLNSHIRE

The Man Who Built America's First Houses

When in May 1607 the band of one hundred or so English colonists landed on the coast of Virginia to establish Jamestown, the first successful and permanent British settlement in America, they naturally faced an absence of the comforts previously enjoyed by even the poorest of them at their homes in England. Initially they even had to continue living aboard their cramped ships or in tents whilst, under the direction of master carpenter William Laxon of Lincolnshire, they constructed a fort for protection and rough huts as temporary accommodation. But these things once done, Laxon turned his energies to what the settlers yearned for most of all after their long and uncomfortable voyage – the provision of (relatively) comfortable permanent dwellings.

Wattle and daub construction in progress

All of us tend to go with what we know and William was no exception, for he employed as his pattern for these, the first English dwellings in America, the design and construction techniques widely popular in his far-away home county. (Apart from that being his place of origin, we sadly know little of him.) Essentially, the houses were constructed of wattle and daub. 'Wattle' is a woven lattice of strips which is covered with the 'daub' – a sticky material usually made of a combination of wet soil, clay, sand, animal dung and straw. These materials had the advantage of being commonly available in or near Jamestown, just as they had been back in Lincolnshire. The wattle and daub walls were framed by timber (preferably oak for longevity) and indeed still are, for wattle and daub structures continue to be erected to this day.

One of Laxon's Lincolnshire-style houses re-constructed in Jamestown

Roofing was by means of thatch, suitable material being available in Jamestown, even if not of the varieties used in England.

The houses consisted of one or two rooms, sometimes with a central chimney as – yet again – was the case back in William Laxon's county of birth. The virtually identical nature of these New and Old World dwellings is immediately apparent in the photographs on preceding page and below, though the walls of the English example illustrated have subsequently been coated with a more enduring surface to minimise maintenance. Many of these Lincolnshire wattle and daub cottages date from William Laxon's own day, and by general consent the best examples are to be found in the village of Thimbleby, a little over a mile from the town of Horncastle.

A traditional Laxon-style wattle-and-daub house in Lincolnshire

How were these new houses furnished, it may be asked? Here we can move from consideration of Jamestown specifically to Colonial America generally, for furniture in the great majority of early homes – wherever built and of whatever style – was initially conspicuous by its absence, for most colonists brought very little of it with them: being bulky, it lost out in competition for limited shipboard space to items such as food, clothing, tents, cooking utensils, crockery, weapons, weaving looms, lanterns, tubs, pails, candles, tools, seeds and agricultural equipment. The tools, of course, provided the settlers with the means to construct on arrival whatever beds, tables, chairs, cupboards, dressers and chests they required, even if initially elegance of appearance had to give way to speed of manufacture. Even so, many folk necessarily lived in somewhat depressing conditions for several years, finding little luxury in their abodes at the end of each day to compensate them for their long hours of toil, for example as farmers. Farming was certainly at the centre of the lives of most, both for the twin purposes of feeding themselves and of earning an income. The work involved, even in areas conducive to agricultural success, was back-breaking and lasted from dawn to dusk: clearing land, tilling virgin soil, digging wells, breeding cattle, sheep and pigs, erecting fencing, constructing barns, planting and gathering crops, milling corn, making wagons and carts, creating primitive roads and tracks and all the rest. Naturally, some of these tasks were best left to specialists whenever possible, whom the farmers rewarded with food and cash – British pounds, shillings and pence - thus forming the primitive basis of a trading economy.

For the luckier or more determined, however, or for those who arrived with a little capital, life could be made tolerably comfortable fairly soon, especially after the emergence of larger-scale immigration in the 1620s onwards. We can gain some idea of what things were like in a fairly prosperous home of the 1630s by, for example, reference to the Dillingham family of the Massachusetts town of Ipswich, for we have been left an account of their home two years after their arrival from old Ipswich in Suffolk, England. Sadly, the account is one compiled by John Dillingham's executors for, despite the relative decency of the accommodation, life in the frontier settlement proved too harsh for him and he died in 1635, to be followed not long afterwards by his wife. The Dillinghams' house, the executors recorded, possessed two rooms plus outbuildings and benefitted from thirty acres of upland, sixty acres of grassland, and six acres of planting ground, of which four were devoted to corn. Apple and other fruit trees and bushes were fenced off in the garden. They owned a horse (a mare), three cows, two bullocks, two heiffers, four calves and four pigs. They had an indentured servant, Thomas

Downs, to help cultivate the land and care for the stock, and a maid Ann Towle – a "faithful servant" – who not only helped with the housework but also worked in the fields.

Though the Dillinghams enjoyed a good social position, they possessed little in the way of fine furniture and their parlour – which had a very large fireplace – was also used as a bedroom, a common practice everywhere in the seventeenth century. (Though not mentioned, there was probably another bedroom in an attic.) The contents of the house principally comprised two bedsteads valued at one pound 6 shillings and eightpence; a cupboard, 10 shillings; a sea chest, 10 shillings; two "joyned Chaires", 5 shillings; a round table, 7 shillings; a "deske", 4 shillings; and a band box, 2 shillings, plus a small nest of boxes worth only 3 shillings. There were feather mattresses, bolsters, pillows and coverlets, with flaxen sheets for Mr. & Mrs. Dillingham's bed and a warming pan to defend them from the cold of winter. Coarse sheets sufficed for the beds of Ann Towle and Thomas Downs but they, poor things, apparently went without the benefit of warming pans. There were probably other items such as benches, stools and shelving of values insufficient to have been worth detailing. There were, also, two small silver bowls and a wide variety of pewter plates and some spoons and knives. There were no table forks, for these were practically unknown in Massachusetts at the time. It is said that the first fork was brought over by Governor Winthrop in 1630 and carefully stored in a case. Knives, spoons and fingers were enough to meet the demands of table manners in the seventeenth century.

For the very, very luckiest, brick houses on the English pattern came on the scene in the late 1630s, and by 1660s economic and manufacturing conditions had developed to the extent that a handful of the elite could afford impressive dwellings. The oldest surviving example is what is nowadays called 'Bacon's Castle', a mansion completed in 1665 by a rich man called Allen, and originally known throughout Virginia as 'Arthur Allen's Brick House' by virtue of its rarity.

Readers with a particular interest in domestic conditions in Colonial America are recommended to read the excellent *Every Day Life in the Massachusetts Bay Colony* by George Francis Dow, from which the above description of the Dillingham household is largely taken.

But, in the meantime, do go to Thimbleby, take a stroll around and, who knows, you may set eyes on a wattle and daub cottage William Laxon himself worked on before he departed for his new life in the New World . . .

LINCOLNSHIRE

John Wesley: the Famous Preacher Who Told Americans "God is Idle"

Many would find it hard to credit that a truly loving God could idly observe human beings' misfortunes and yet stubbornly resist lifting a divine finger to help them. And yet that, stripped of theological niceties, is the message that was preached to Britons and to their fellow colonists in America by none other than by ardent Christian John Wesley, the founder of Methodism. We have Wesley's word for it: "God does nothing except in response to believing prayer".

Wesley was born in the small Lincolnshire village of Epworth in 1703, the fifteenth of the nineteen children of Rector Samuel Wesley and his wife Susanna (who, poor woman, must surely have tended her flock more pro-actively than her son John reckoned God tended his). Epworth was a poor and isolated settlement and few of its residents were literate. Rector Samuel, a kind man, did what he could to ameliorate their lot. However, his religious views were not entirely mainstream and in 1709 the rectory was burned down in an arson attack by a Christian opponent. Fortunately, all the occupants escaped – six-year-old John being rescued from a first-floor window. It was as a result of this incident that Susanna, echoing a biblical phrase about Israel, famously referred to John Wesley as "a brand plucked from the burning". The rectory was soon re-built in Queen Anne style and stands to this day, a large and elegant Grade One Listed Building, testimony to the fact that however poor the villagers were, their rector and his family lived in considerable style.

Epworth Rectory, now owned by a Methodist Board of Trustees

However, the replacement rectory was also to come under attack, though this time from a different opponent and a supernatural one at that – to wit, a poltergeist, one of the most famous in British history. Wesley family letters record with a wealth of detail the mysterious, frightening noises they experienced – groanings, knockings, bangings, thumpings and other un-nerving manifestations. Daughter Hetty named the ghost "Old Jeffrey" after a former caretaker, and one of Old Jeffrey's most memorable performances took place on Christmas Day 1716. In Susanna Wesley's words, "there was such a noise in the room over our heads, as if several people were walking, then running up and down stairs that we thought the children would be frightened . . ." Old Jeffrey then excelled himself by "rattling and thundering in every room and even blowing an invisible horn at deafening volume", thus presumably ensuring the Wesley family's Christmas was a memorable one, albeit not in the way they would have wished.

By the time of these alleged paranormal events, John Wesley was attending Charterhouse School, then quartered in Smithfield, London. On leaving Charterhouse he transferred to Christ Church College at Oxford University, from which he graduated Master of Arts in 1625. Shortly afterwards he was ordained as a deacon of the Anglican Church and became a Fellow of another Oxford college, Lincoln (so called because it was founded by a Bishop of Lincoln – in other words, a man from Wesley's 'home turf'). There Wesley taught Greek and lectured on the New Testament, leading a life marked by a rigorous commitment to routine and self-discipline, especially in relation to all matters religious. However, his time at Lincoln College was interrupted when in 1629 his father asked him to go back to Lincolnshire to assist him by undertaking a stint as curate at Wroote, a parish adjoining Epworth. He spent two years in the role before resuming his former duties at the College. His younger brother Charles had by now had also arrived there as an undergraduate, and the pair quickly formed a close theological alliance. Charles and a handful of others, John found, had already formed a small group devoted to religious study and the pursuit of devout Christian living; John became a member and, soon, its leader.

Memorial statue of John Wesley, Savannah, Georgia

The group met daily on the dot at six in the morning for three hours of prayers, psalm recitals and Bible reading. Every waking hour, on the hour, they prayed for several minutes, routinely fasted for two specified days a week and took communion on all fifty-two Sundays of the year, even though the Church required this to be done on only three. (John went so far as to draw up a chart to record his spiritual activities hour-by-hour, even ranking his hourly "temper of devotion" on a scale of 1 to 9.) In short, the members of the group were truly *methodical* – from which the terms *Methodism* and the *Methodist Church* were ultimately to be derived. Their practices drew attention in an Oxford University not marked at this time by a universal enthusiasm for religion. Thus the Wesleys and their companions soon became mockingly known as the Holy Club. A popular ditty sprung up:

> *"By rule they eat, by rule they drink,*
> *By rule they do all things but think.*
> *Accuse the priests of loose behaviour*
> *To get more in the laymen's favour.*
> *Method alone must guide 'em all*
> *When 'Methodists' themselves they call."*

But devoted as the Holy Club was to religious matters, its members did not overlook the practical needs of less fortunate folk, for they visited prisoners in jail, relieved debtors and ministered to the sick, activities whose worthiness naturally enhanced the Methodists' reputation amongst the needy. Theologically, and despite the intellectual mockery aimed at them in Oxford, the Methodists' reputation as dedicated Christians spread in wider circles. In 1735 this led to John Wesley being invited to serve as a missionary to Native Americans – 'Red Indians' as they were then known – in the British North American colony of Georgia. The invitation was extended by the Society for the Propagation of the Gospel in Foreign Parts and Wesley seized it eagerly, viewing it as an opportunity to save his own soul by preaching his brand of Christianity to a people uncontaminated by – as Wesley saw it – impure versions peddled by others. That Wesley viewed this opportunity in the New World as of seminal importance is borne out by the fact that a description of his time there comprised the opening section of the journal of his life which he published later. It is probable, too, that the prominence he gave it reflected his desire to defend his record there, for all did not go well.

To assist him in Georgia, he took with him his brother Charles and his friends Charles Delamotte and Bernard Ingham. They sailed on *The Simmonds* from Gravesend and disembarked in Savannah in February 1736. Their fellow passengers included a group of Moravians, members of a movement founded in Bohemia (now part of the Czech Republic) in the mid-1400s. Moravians contended that formal membership of a congregation was "for no one a substitute for a personal encounter with the Saviour". Wesley was mightily impressed by the Moravians aboard *The Simmonds* when, in the course of a storm so violent everyone else panicked, they calmly prayed and sang hymns. From this point onwards he began to incorporate numerous Moravian tenets into his own thinking.

Georgia, named in honour of King George II, had been established only four years earlier and was the last of the original thirteen colonies. Unsurprisingly, there was a shortage of clergy in the infant colony and the grand plan of converting Native Americans was soon de facto abandoned in favour of ministering to the religiously-deprived colonists themselves. In thus transferring the object of his attentions he was much encouraged by the colony's founder, George Oglethorpe of Godalming in Surrey.

However, Wesley soon ran into difficulties. First, he found himself in the crossfire of disputes between Oglethorpe and Savannah's chief magistrate, a man called Thomas Causton. Causton made life difficult for Wesley because of his (Wesley's) continuing loyalty to Oglethorpe, and the ensuing antipathy between missionary and magistrate was exacerbated by Causton's deceitful financial dealings with Wesley's admired Moravians. Second, Wesley apparently found it difficult to cope with the distances he had to travel to perform his duties, which is surprising in light of the peripatetic preaching across the length and breadth of England which in the end was to become the hallmark of his life. Third, he seemed in Georgia unable to establish that remarkable rapport with 'the man and woman in the street' which, again, he was so triumphantly to achieve later. Probably it was because – being the product of a sophisticated and urban society in Oxford – he found little in common with men and women struggling to make their way in an alien, largely rural world. Fourth, though the overwhelming majority of the colonists were British, there were also in this particular area Portugese, Germans and Swiss and the language barrier proved hard to overcome. Finally – and possibly for some of the same reasons as John – brother Charles was largely rejected by the settlers in Fort Frederica to whom he had been appointed chaplain. Consequently, in less than a year after arriving in the New World, Charles abandoned Georgia and his brother and sailed back to England, never to set foot in the colony again.

Perhaps most significantly, there had been what we might call 'woman trouble'. On arrival, Wesley had written in his diary, "At my first coming to Savannah . . . I was determined to have no intimacy with any woman in America" but only a week or two later he informed brother Charles that some of the colonists were "women, younger, refined, God-fearing. Pray that I know none of them after the flesh." Clearly, Wesley was feeling the stirrings of love and lust, for which he condemned himself just as much as he condemned other human beings for his and their folly in being human and possessing human desires. His words imply that not even devotion to Christianity was proof against what the Church called 'unlawful sexual intercourse' – and of course we know that in many instances it was not.

The chief target of John Wesley's interest was a 17-year-old called Sophia Hopkey. "Her words," he wrote, "her eyes, her air, her every motion and gesture [are] full of such a softness and sweetness!" Unsurprisingly, he concluded it was his duty to give Sophia frequent religious and secular instruction. He was soon to record that at the end of one lesson he "took her by the hand and, before we parted, kissed". He wrote sensually of his pleasure in encircling her waist and many a dalliance ensued between the two. Whether or not things ever went further than enthusiastic canoodling, we do not know, though Wesley was later to vigorously deny it. That Sophia was ever a willing partner is certainly clear, for she re-assured him that if he visited her house, they could be alone – "We may be in the garden, or under [sic] the shed or anywhere."

Pertinently, Sophia was the niece of Thomas Causton who, as noted earlier, was later to become Wesley's bete noire. But at this time her family expressed themselves in favour of her becoming Wesley's wife. However, after a liaison of many months, and declarations by Sophia that Wesley could trust her – "I shall never deceive you" – Sophia jilted Wesley without warning. The news was broken to him by Sophia's mother, who one morning simply announced to him that Sophia had engaged herself to be married to a young man named William Williamson – and would Wesley as their priest please publish the marriage banns the following Sunday! Wesley was devastated: "To see her no more! That thought was the piercings of a sword. It was not to be borne – nor shaken off. I was weary of the world, of light, of life . . . I did seek after God but I found him not . . . I could not pray. Then indeed the snares of death were about me, the pains of hell overtook me." It is impossible to do other than feel deeply for him in his misery.

However, Wesley's emotions of sorrow soon transmuted themselves into what many might perceive as feelings of jealous revenge: he was, of course, still Sophia's parish priest and in that capacity he took the profoundly unwise decision to refuse her Holy Communion on the grounds that she was a deceitful woman. In the religious context of the day, this was a devastating act. Sophia's husband and father immediately responded by instituting legal proceedings against Wesley for dereliction of duty and in December 1737 the devout Methodist fled Georgia, virtually a fugitive from justice. As in the case of his brother Charles, he was never to return. Back in Lincolnshire, he gradually re-established himself as a man and a Christian believer and went on to become possibly the most famous and persuasive preacher since the Reformation. His name will forever be indelibly linked with the creation of the Methodist Church.

Despite his unhappy and desperately unproductive period in Georgia, Wesley's ghost – if he has one – must surely take more than a little satisfaction that over time his influence, if not his person, was to return and pervade the New World from which he had so ignominiously departed to the extent that the Methodist Church in the USA today has more than 8 million members . . .

LINCOLNSHIRE

The First Governor of America's Smallest State and "the Woman More Bold Than a Man"

Geographically, Rhode Island is the smallest state in the USA and also one of the least populous. Boasting little more than a million inhabitants it is, however, vastly larger than the hamlet of Marston in Lincolnshire from which its first Governor hailed – even today that hamlet is home to fewer than 400 souls. The Marston child who was to become that Governor was one William Coddington, born in the year 1601. His life was to become inter-twined with another remarkable emigrant who had taken her first breath a few years' earlier, one Anne Hutchinson of Alford in the same county.

William was the son of Robert Coddington, a prosperous yeoman (a man holding and cultivating a small estate) and his wife Margaret. The younger Coddington, it seems, was well-educated, for we know from his surviving correspondence that he was highly literate and possessed an excellent knowledge of the law. He married at the age of nineteen and his wife Mary (whose surname was probably Burt) gave birth to two sons; sadly, the babies died almost immediately – not at all an uncommon misfortune at that time of still-primitive medical knowledge. No doubt William withstood the blow philosophically and ascribed it to the will of God, for he was a deeply-committed Puritan. In 1625, when Coddington was twenty-three, King Charles I came to the throne; this was not a cause for celebration on the part of Coddington and his fellow-thinkers, for the new monarch was a closet-Catholic and thus at the other end of the religious spectrum.

In 1627 King Charles I desperately needed money – as he was to do so often in his reign – for in the preceding year Parliament had refused to make him any grant at all. He therefore called on his subjects to give him money directly, "lovingly, freely and voluntarily" – a trio of adjectives which soon proved hopelessly optimistic, for the great majority of citizens refused to pay. The King's only recourse therefore was to institute a system of forced loans – though 'loan' was rightly considered a misnomer, for few believed that they would live to see their money returned. Anyone who refused to contribute was threatened with punishment and the King thus succeeded in raking in about £250,000. However, not a few stalwarts held out, amongst them William Coddington. Unlike some, he was not imprisoned for his failure to pay and we do not know what, if any, penalty was imposed on him. But we can be certain that the affair contributed to his disenchantment with the religious climate in England, especially as the King had encouraged Church of England ministers to preach in favour of the people giving him their money. (The Church of England, of course, was only marginally less popular with Puritans than was Roman Catholicism.)

William Coddington

Coddington's disenchantment continued to fester and three years' later, in 1630, he and wife Mary decided to leave Lincolnshire to join Governor John Winthrop and his party in establishing new lives in Boston, Massachusetts. Coddington soon established himself there as a successful merchant and also assumed a prominent role in civic life, for Winthrop had appointed him as his principal assistant even before their departure from England. The two men initially continued to get on well together but difficulties soon ensued, for Coddington – in common with not a few others – quickly fell under the influence of the charismatic Anne Hutchinson (to whom the reader was introduced in the opening paragraph).

Anne, her husband and family had arrived in the new Boston from her Lincolnshire birthplace in 1634, when she was aged about forty. She was well-educated and had been much impressed by the sermons given by John Cotton in St. Botolph's Church in the English Boston. In the American Boston she held meetings in her house (built by her husband just across the street from Governor Winthrop's) in which she forcefully advocated Cotton's views and soon succeeded in recruiting the moneyed Coddington as an enthusiastic supporter. This triggered religious schism between him and his mentor Winthrop, for Winthrop abhorred Anne, describing her thus: "[a] woman of haughty and fierce carriage, of a nimble wit and active spirit, and a very voluble tongue, more bold than a man". What gave Winthrop and the majority of Puritans particular cause for concern about this feisty woman were her views on the salvation of the soul. She argued that the Puritan hierarchy's emphasis on a person's good works as the way to salvation was gravely mistaken and in conflict with true Puritan teachings. Salvation, she maintained, could come from God's grace alone. Thus arose in the new Boston another instance of the religious strife which besmirched the New World, despite the conviction of so many that 'over there' religion would somehow attain a free and uniform perfection. (It might be remarked that the capacity of religious persons, then as now, to 'know' God's views and to condemn, as wrong or evil, rivals who 'know' differently, can rarely be overestimated.)

Central to Anne Hutchinson's story is the fact that she was yet another of those people who, allegedly, are privileged to have heart-to-heart chats with the Creator, he (she said) being kind enough in her case to assure her that she was capable of interpreting the Scriptures without his help! Naturally, this was seen as heretical by the new Boston's Puritan establishment who believed that the ultimate religious authority was the Bible (as interpreted by them, of course). Her notoriety was compounded by the fact that she was perceived as an obstreperous woman in a male-dominated society.

Put on civil trial on charges of sedition in November 1637, she displayed no desire to mollify her accusers. Indeed, in a tactic not likely to be recommended by modern defence counsel she threatened the judges with a Divine curse. But this did not shake them, and nor did anything they said shake her. She calmly maintained her claim that God spoke to her directly and this, the Court decided, amounted to blasphemy. Her admirer Coddington was fearless enough to stand up and assert the unpopular contrary – that there was "no law of God that she hath broken nor any law of the country that she hath broke . . ." Unsurprisingly, though, Coddington was ignored and Governor Winthrop delivered the damning verdict: "Mrs. Hutchinson, the sentence of the Court you hear is that you are banished from out of our jurisdiction as a woman not fit for our society, and are to be imprisoned till the Court shall send you away". She had stood little chance from the outset, for even John Cotton, her inspirer, describing the meetings at her house as a "promiscuous and filthy coming together of men and women . . ."

A campaign of intimidation against her followers swiftly ensued and many recanted, but a group of loyalists resolved to flee with her. Amongst this group was Coddington, who was elected as organiser; under his guidance preparations were made to depart for Aquidneck Island (later to be re-named Rhode Island), which he had accumulated enough wealth to purchase. Paradoxically, despite her sentence of exile, Anne Hutchinson was not free to accompany her adherents for some time, for she was held in prison pending a second trial, on this occasion in the Ecclesiastical Court. When the Court convened four months' later, the men of the Church cheerily topped-up her civil punishment by excommunicating her religiously, thus rendering her to their great satisfaction not only homeless but Godless. "For as much as you, Mrs. Hutchinson, have highly transgressed and offended . . . and troubled the Church with your Errors and have drawn away many a poor Soule and have upheld your Revelations; and for as much as you have made a Lie . . . therefore in the name of our Lord Jesus Christ . . . I do cast you out and deliver you up to Satan . . . and account you from this time to be a Heathen and a Publican . . . I command you in the name of Christ Jesus and of this Church as a Leper to withdraw yourselfe out of the Congregation."

Upon her expulsion, Hutchinson and her family joined Coddington and the rest in the new settlement of Pocasset, soon to be re-named Portsmouth. Shortly after her arrival there after a long trek through snow, Anne, even though approaching fifty and already the mother of a dozen or so children, gave birth to another infant, or possibly multiple infants, all sadly malformed and stillborn. Winthrop was exultant: "She brought forth not one but thirty [sic] monstrous births or thereabouts . . . see how the wisdom of God fitted this judgement to her sin every way, for look – as she had misshapen opinions, so she must bring forth deformed monsters".

The reader may not be surprised to learn that this was not the last of her misfortunes, for the new settlement was soon itself riven by rifts and difficulties. Coddington, it was alleged, was autocratic and certain it is that he began to alienate numerous of his fellow settlers, including Anne herself. The upshot was Coddington's overthrow and his departure with yet another split-off group to the southern end of the island, where he established the settlement of Newport.

But in a further twist there came about an almost fairy-tale reconciliation, for in 1640 the towns of Portsmouth and Newport agreed to re-unite peacefully, and elected Coddington as Governor of the whole colony. He served in this capacity for seven years and remained prominent in Rhode Island's affairs until his death, though the latter part of his life continued to be marked by complicated twists and turns, controversies, achievements and disappointments.

Nevertheless, he was re-elected Deputy Governor or Governor several times, the final occasion being in 1677. He was not to enjoy the position for long, however, for he died in the November of 1678.

What of the fate of Anne? Her end, sadly, came long before Coddington's. In the summer of 1642 she had moved to New York, accompanied by seven of her children, a son-in-law and half-a-dozen or so servants. They settled in northern Bronx, not far from what was to become known as the Hutchinson River. Her timing was not of the best, for mistreatment by the Dutch governor had raised the ire of the local Siwanoy tribe of Native Americans. The terrible fate at their hands which befell Hutchinson and her little clan in August of the following year is described by her modern biographer, Eve La Plante: "The Siwanoy warriors stampeded into the tiny settlement . . . prepared to burn down every house . . . the Siwanoy seized and scalped Francis Hutchinson, William Collins and several servants, the two Annes (mother and daughter), and the younger children, William, Katherine, Mary and Zuriel . . . one of Hutchinson's daughters, seeking to escape, was caught as she was getting over a hedge and they drew her back again by the hair of her head to the stump of a tree, and there cut off her head with a hatchet."

The Siwanoy then dragged the bodies into the house and set it ablaze. There was one survivor, nine-year-old daughter Susanna who had been out gathering blueberries. She was discovered by the Siwanoys hiding in Split Rock, a crevice nearby. Either because their blood-lust was sated or because they were intrigued by her red hair – which they would have considered highly unusual – the attackers spared her life and hauled her away captive. She was kept by them for several years until ransomed back to some relatives who still lived in Boston.

One might have thought that when the dreadful news of the killings reached them, even Anne's religious opponents might have felt a touch of pity, but not a bit of it. The Reverend Thomas Weld wrote: "I never heard that the Indians in those parts did ever before this commit the like outrage upon any one family or families; and therefore God's hand is more apparently seen herein to pick out this woeful woman". Pastor Peter Bulkley wrote: "Let her damned heresies and the just vengeance of God, by which she perished, terrify all her seduced followers . . ." Not to be outdone, Governor Winthrop (he who said "we shall be as a shining city set upon a hill") referred to her as an "American Jezebel" and recorded: "Thus it hath pleased the Lord to have compassion on his poor churches here and to discover this great impostor, an instrument of Satan so fitted and trained to his service for interrupting the [triumph] of his kingdom in this part of the world".

There really were some nice people amongst those early English settlers in America, were there not?

LINCOLNSHIRE AND CAMBRIDGESHIRE

The Pilgrim Fathers At Home: Gainsborough and Scrooby

The core group of the Pilgrim Fathers – that small but illustrious band of Puritans who left England for America in 1620 – came from the little town of Gainsborough in Lincolnshire and the village of Scrooby, which lies about a dozen miles to the west of it (technically, just over the border with Northampton). Both places are within easy reach of the Lincolnshire seaport of Boston, central to the whole Pilgrim story. The most significant member of the group was William Brewster, for in Massachusetts he was to become the Religious Elder of Plymouth Colony and founder of the festival of Thanksgiving, universally observed by Americans to this day. He is, in short, generally considered to be the most famous of all the Pilgrims.

Brewster was born in Scrooby in 1566. His father was Receiver and Bailiff of the Archbishop of York's manor house there and also Master of the Queen's Posts, responsible for the safety of the Crown Messengers on their journeys from London to Scotland. The Brewster family lived in a wing of the magnificent mansion, which at that time comprised 39 rooms, part of which remains standing to this day. As a youth, William was sent to study at Peterhouse College, Cambridge University, a hotbed of Puritan-leaning religious reform. On graduation he entered the office of William Davison, assistant to Queen Elizabeth's Secretary of State and crafty spymaster, Francis Walsingham, where he acquired some political and diplomatic experience – the only Pilgrim to do so. On one occasion he took part in an official mission to the more religiously-tolerant Netherlands and there made contact with local Puritans who strongly encouraged him in his radical views. But when Davison lost the Queen's favour and with it his position in 1587, Brewster perforce returned to Scrooby. From time to time he did venture away, notably to act as a priest at Lincoln Cathedral from 1600 to 1602, only to be dismissed because his preaching became "dangerous".

Peterhouse College, Cambridge,
the oldest of the University's colleges and where
William Brewster was an undergraduate

Back in Scrooby, having become irreedeemably devoted to his heretical views (as the Anglican Church perceived them), Brewster began to absent himself from services at St. Wilfrid's Church, where he had been baptised and had traditionally worshipped with his parents and siblings. For this he was severely reprimanded in the Ecclesiastical Court. However, he had by this time gathered around him a small but stalwart band of village sympathisers – popularly called 'Scroobyites' – and nothing the Church authorities could do was to stand in his or their way. Thus it was that in 1607 the Scroobyites made their first attempt to find religious tolerance overseas by fleeing to the Netherlands.

The remaining part of Scrooby Manor House,
William Brewster's home

Here we must introduce another of Brewster's allies, the prominent preacher, John Smyth of Gainsborough. He was the leader of a group of like-minded thinkers in the town and, like Brewster, was to become an eminent Pilgrim Father. Smyth and his flock were strong proponents of "believers' baptism" – the baptism of adults willing to make a conscious decision to "follow God" rather than the baptism of infants with no awareness. Brewster was amongst those who witnessed Smyth's adult re-baptism on March 24th 1606. Another of those present was Dr. John Clifford and he has left us this description: " . . . this night at midnight elder John Morton baptised John Smyth, vicar of Gainsborough, in the River Don. It was so dark we were obliged to have torch lights. Elder Brewster prayed, Mister Smyth made a good confession; walked to Epworth [another nearby Lincolnshire village] in his cold clothes but received no harm. The distance was over two miles. All of our friends were present. To the triune God be praise."

St. Wilfrid's Church, Scrooby:
William Brewster first worshipped there, then boycotted it

Smyth went on to frequently preach at one of the most magnificent buildings in Lincolnshire, Gainsborough Old Hall, the home of the Hickman family. The Hickmans were themselves strong non-conformists and only too happy to give Smyth – and Brewster – succour and shelter there. Lady Rose Hickman, writing in 1610, recorded that the family had held "unsound" religious views for many a long day: "My mother in the dayes of King Henry VIII came to some light of the gospel by means of some English books sent privately to her by my father's factor from beyond the sea: where upon she used to call me with my two sisters into her chamber to read us out of these same good books very privately for fear of trouble because these good books were then accepted hereticall . . ."

Magnificent Gainsborough Old Hall,
with its wealth of Pilgrim Father associations

Many of the Gainsborough folk who gathered to worship with Smyth at the Old Hall joined with his Scroobyites to become Pilgrims. The magnificent dwelling is thus at the heart of the Pilgrim Fathers' story and intensely evocative it is to re-live their experiences here. You can do it for yourself by standing in the Great Hall (the Old Hall's principal chamber) and imagining the graceful presence of Lady Rose, her family and servants, the excited yet respectful chatter of the welcomes extended to William Brewster; and, perhaps above all, by bringing to life in your mind the sight and sound of John Smyth preaching to his congregation – men, women and children all virtually unknown then, world-famous today.

LINCOLNSHIRE

The Pilgrim Fathers and the *Original* Boston

From way distant across the flatlands of The Fens, today's traveller cannot fail to be impressed by the massive church tower dominating the seaport town of Boston in Lincolnshire. Known by the affectionate and mock-derogatory name of "The Stump", the tower rises high above St. Botolph's, the largest parish church in England. And when a traveller rests his or her eyes on that ancient and beautiful building, knowingly or unknowingly he or she steps back four centuries in time to share a view long ago enjoyed by the most famous of all emigrants to America, the Pilgrim Fathers. For it was from Boston that the Pilgrim Fathers began the journey which ultimately was to take them to the New World. 'Boston' is a contraction of 'St. Botolph's Town' and it is after this old Boston in Lincolnshire that the new city of Boston in Massachusetts is named.

The "Stump" of St. Botolph's, viewed from the river

From at least the twelfth century onwards, old Boston was a centre of trade with mainland Europe and by the mid-1500s its citizens were importing not only physical goods from the Continent but something else, invisible yet fundamental: the intellectual and religious creed of Calvinism, the basis of the Puritan revolt against the Pope and Roman Catholicism. The creed was to revolutionise the Christian thinking not only of Bostonians but also of large numbers of their fellow citizens in neighbouring counties.

Many of Calvinism's adherents became known as Puritans, consequent upon their belief that they – and they alone – were following a *pure* form of Christianity after centuries of sin, distortion and error on the part of traditional Church hierarchies. Away with vestments, away with ritual, away with devious priests, away with the anti-Christ (the Pope), were the cries. And though in many eyes these demands had been met in the time of King Henry VIII and subsequently, and though England was by now officially a Protestant nation, many worshippers were convinced that reform had not gone nearly far enough. In their adamant view, pernicious and sinful Romish practices still suffused the Church and nation, constituting an unforgiveable affront to the Lord. Consequently, for Puritans, simplicity of life and worship and (as they saw it) true obedience to the word of God were still unattained objectives. This failure they were determined to put right. "Separatists" – real Puritan hard-liners – believed this could not be done from inside the Church but only by the creation of a separate movement, and the most hard-line of these Separatists did not believe it could be done in England at all. To succeed, they were convinced, they would have to seek new lives in more congenial lands. In short, they would have to become 'Pilgrims'. Thus it was that from the seaport of old Boston in 1607 that the small cadre of men, women and children (about thirty people in all) who were to form the inner core of the famous Pilgrims made their first attempt to escape overseas.

The members of the group came from Gainsborough in Lincolnshire and nearby Scrooby, both of which lay within easy distance of Boston. The most prominent of the group, in terms of lasting historical reputation, were William Bradford and Elder

William Brewster. Brewster was head of the congregation and Bradford's particular fame lies in the fact that he was to become Governor of Plymouth Colony in Massachusetts – the Pilgrim Fathers' settlement – a position he held for more than thirty years. Bradford, Brewster and the rest gathered in the port of old Boston for two reasons: first, and obviously, it gave them access to shipping and, second, many Bostonians had sympathy for their anti-establishment views.

Boston Guildhall

The plan was to move lock, stock and barrel to the Netherlands, specifically to Amsterdam. The Netherlands were the destination of choice for the reason that a far more tolerant form of Protestantism predominated there than in England, and indeed not a few English Puritans had already established themselves in that country. In Boston, the latest little group of would-be emigrants were therefore delighted when they made contact with the master of a small ship who (naturally in return for cash) promised to transport them across the North Sea to their Dutch destination. We do not know the name of that shipmaster, nor whether he was an Englishman or a Netherlander. Neither do we know if he was aware from the outset that his passengers were religious refugees, or whether he locked on to the fact only after they had boarded. Either way, he was exposing himself to severe punishment from the English authorities, for assisting such 'heretics' to flee was a serious offence. What we do know is that he very rapidly betrayed them, for the vessel was almost immediately intercepted in Scotia Creek, a mere three or so miles from its departure point. (There is a memorial on the river bank marking the location.) The would-be escapees were seized, arrested and brought back to Boston in open boats. There they were thrown into prison in the town's Guildhall

The two cells in the Guildhall may be visited to this day; they are small – each about seven feet by five-and-a-half feet – and it is likely that only the men were kept in them. The women and children were given free range in the kitchen area, though the women complained that they were "searched to their shirts". The women and children were soon set free but the seven men were incarcerated for about a month. On appearing before the magistrate in the courtroom on the floor above (which can also be visited) they were, however, released on bail to appear at Lincoln Assizes. However, they failed to surrender to bail, no doubt certain that their duty to God was infinitely greater than their obligation to the authorities. No serious attempt was made to track them down and re-seize them, however, and this we must attribute to the Bostonians' sympathy for their views referred to earlier.

A re-enactor in one of the Boston Guildhall cells

A year later, the little band made a second attempt to reach the Netherlands, this time successfully. There they dwelt in Leiden for twelve years before returning to England and embarking on the *Mayflower* for the New World. Thus, if you visit Boston Guildhall you visit the site of the very first step in the Pilgrim Fathers' epic journey.

We cannot ourselves leave Boston without considering another Boston figure of prime importance in the history of Britain's American colonies: a 29-year-old graduate of Trinity College, Cambridge, the Reverend John Cotton, a man deeply sympathetic to the new religious thought. He was appointed as vicar of St. Botolph's in 1612 but, contrary to the Pilgrims, he wanted to stay in his native land and change the church from within. He succeeded in maintaining his rebellious position at St. Botolph's for twenty years, thanks to supportive aldermen on Boston town council, lenient bishops and to a capacity for diplomacy which sprang from his conciliatory and gentle demeanour. In that time he preached hundreds if not thousands of contentious sermons from the wonderful and still-surviving pulpit.

The magnificent pulpit in St.Botolph's
from which John Cotton preached

Curiously, despite his own antagonism to authority, Cotton had a deep distrust of popular opinion: "Democracy, I do not conceive that ever God did ordain as a fit government for church or commonwealth. If the people be governors, who shall be governed?" As in so many other instances from yesterday and today, does this amount to little more than saying, "People should believe as I believe, do as I say, conduct themselves as I conduct myself." "Toleration", he also said, "made the world anti-Christian" – though toleration was what his fellow Puritans, the Pilgrim Fathers had left England to obtain! (Consistency has, of course, never been a priority in religious matters – or indeed in many other spheres.)   Neither did Cotton demonstrate any regard for the views of women: "She is but a woman and many dangerous and unsound principles are held by her."

Eventually, however, the tolerance of the Church for Cotton's apostasy evaporated and in 1632 the hard-line Bishop of London, William Laud, summoned him to appear before the Court of High Commission. Cotton immediately perceived that his time was at an end and went into hiding. A year later he too succeeded in escaping from the old Boston to its new namesake in the New World, where his fame went before him and ensured his prompt appointment as the head of the First Church. He was to hold the position for many years and exercise enormous influence over the religious life of the colony, including helping to frame the fundamental laws of Massachusetts, many of which remain in force to this day.

And, perhaps, in the New World he was forced to develop a little more sympathy for the concept of democracy – perhaps, even, for the status of women!

NORFOLK

America's First Doctor

Many things are vital when you face a 3,000 mile voyage across a vast and unpredictable ocean on a sailing vessel barely 100 feet long. But when the Pilgrim Fathers' *Maflower* left England carrying the 130 or so men, women and children to be deposited upon the wild and alien North American shore, few things were more important than the services of a doctor – even if, in 1620, the knowledge and skills of any medical man, however eminent, were sadly limited and his medicines and equipment commensurately primitive.

At that time, most doctors still believed that bodily health was governed by four 'humours' or fluids – blood, phlegm, yellow bile and black bile, and that illness arose from the excess or deficiency of one or more of them. But progress was being made – the thermometer had been invented, some effective remedies were available (for example, quinine to treat malaria) and, of course, surgical procedures, though brutal, were relatively well-practised, mainly as a result of centuries of war (though the caveat must be entered that surgeons were usually barbers and looked down upon by their medical brethren).

Faith in doctors certainly existed, though, and the presence of a doctor in hazardous times was essential for morale, absence of one devastating to it. Thus, the Pilgrim Fathers were careful to ensure that a doctor was aboard the *Mayflower*, one who (if he himself survived) was willing and able to remain in the New World and to continue his ministrations there. In the case of the Pilgrims, the burden fell upon one of their own, a man by the name of Dr. Samuel Fuller who had been born in 1580 in the village of Redenhall in Norfolk. He was the son of a butcher, which possibly gave him some very primitive insights into surgical matters; it may also have given rise to some black humour amongst any Puritans prepared to indulge in such frivolity.

*St. Mary's Church, Redenhall, Norfolk,
in which America's first doctor was baptised*

Fuller was baptised in St. Mary's Church in Redenhall and in adulthood married a woman called Sarah Dunthorne. They were members of the core group of Pilgrims which initially sought sanctuary in the Netherlands, where, unfortunately, Sarah died. He married again, to a woman called Agnes Carpenter but she too was soon to die, in childbirth together with the baby. He married for a third time, to Bridget Lee, by whom he had a daughter but he initially left them behind in the Netherlands whilst he crossed to the New World and became the first doctor ever to be recorded as practising there. He did take with him his servant, William Butten, only for him too to expire on the voyage despite Samuel doing for him all that his limited knowledge permitted. (One can truly say, death was a harsh ruler in the 1600s.)

The *Mayflower*'s Atlantic voyage took over three months, passengers and crew somehow clinging to hope while enduring unimaginably cramped and harsh conditions and being cruelly buffeted by strong westerly gales. Their November landing was only the start of further trials, for that month heralded the start of the cold and cruel New England winter which was to bring on the deaths of almost half of the little group of colonists. Notwithstanding this, Samuel's caring treatment was much appreciated and, as time passed, his reputation became such as he was often called on to assist colonists elsewhere – for example, at Salem in 1629 and Charlestown in 1630.

Although denounced as a 'quack' by one Plymouth man with a reputation for troublemaking, the public as a whole clearly valued highly Samuel's kindness and abilities, for on Samuel's own death in the summer of 1633 Nathaniel Morton, prominent Pilgrim, Colony Secretary and historian, wrote: ". . . Samuel Fuller then died, after he had much helped others, and was a comfort to them; he was their surgeon and physician and did much good in his place, being not only useful in his faculty but otherwise, as he was a Godly man and served Christ in his office of a deacon of the church for many years and forward to do good in his place, and was much missed after God removed him from this world."

Limited though Samuel Fuller's skills may have been, surely few of us can hope for a better epitaph than one which records that we tried to help our fellow beings.

NORFOLK

The Girls from Great Yarmouth and The Witches of Salem

New Englanders can "neither drive a bargain nor make a jest without a text of Scripture at the end on it," reported a visitor in 1680s. In reality, the impact of religion was a good deal more serious than that, for religious mania and fear of the Devil was rife. When no less a person than a new Governor, William Phips, arrived from England in 1692, he hastened to report back to London that his territory was "miserably harassed with a most Horrible Witchcraft or Possession of Devils which had broken upon several Towns. Some scores of poor people were taken with preternatural torments, some scalded with brimstone, some had pins stuck in their flesh, others hurried into the fire and water, and some dragged out of their houses and carried over the tops of trees and hills for many miles".

For this information he relied, he said, on "the loud cries and clamours of the friends of the afflicted people and the advice of the Deputy Governor and many others." Even though he was not convinced of the truth of what he was told and was to have many regrets later, the fact remained that the prisons "were full of people committed upon the suspicion of witchcraft". In light of this he felt compelled to bow to intense popular pressure and establish a special court to try and, if appropriate, punish the malefactors; the alternative was to face a possible breakdown in public order.

Numerous places were affected but the epicentre of the hysteria was the village of Salem, now infamous in history for the trials held there consequent upon Phips's decision to invoke the judicial process. The village was a burgeoning farming centre on the northern edge of Salem town (nowadays re-named Danvers), a prosperous port at that time and boasting a population of about

2,000. Many Salemites were native-born but many, too, were relatively new arrivals from England. Amongst the latter were Rebecca Towne, born in 1621 and her sister Mary, born in 1634. Both were from Great Yarmouth in the county of Norfolk, from which their parents William and Joanna Towne had emigrated in 1640. Another sister, Sarah, was born four years after her parents' arrival in Salem.

The Towne memorial plaque in
St. Nicholas Minster, Great Yarmouth

The troubles in which the three sisters were to be tragically caught up commenced in January 1692 when nine-year-old Elizabeth Parris, the daughter of Salem's minister, the Reverend Samuel Parris, and Parris's niece, 11-year-old Abigail Williams, started having 'fits'. They screamed uncontrollably, threw objects across rooms, uttered animal noises and other peculiar sounds, and writhed and contorted their bodies violently. Soon, many other young girls started to exhibit similar symptoms. A local doctor, William Griggs, confidently diagnosed the origin of the problem as witchcraft. The girls avidly confirmed the 'fact' and initially accused three women of causing their bewitchment: the Parris family's black slave, Tituba, a homeless beggar called Sarah Good, and a poor elderly woman called Sarah Osborn. This was but the beginning, for the number of girls and women falling prey to the contagion and the number accused of causing it, escalated rapidly; no-one, however respectable or 'Godly', could assume themselves free from fear of allegation. Even a four-year-old girl was accused of being a witch. Eventually, twenty people were executed, all but one by hanging on what became known as Gallows Hill. Five others, including two infant children, died while being held in prison.

Amongst the unlucky ranks of the many who soon joined Tituba the slave, Sarah Good and Sarah Osborn as putative witches were the three Towne sisters. Indictments and trials ensued. Of the frail Rebecca Towne, now 71 years old, it was recorded: "The Sheriff brought the witch up the broad aisle [of the courtroom], her chains clanking as she stepped". As in the case of every person accused of demonology, she was not permitted the assistance of a lawyer, though a bold denial of the charge came from her own lips: "I am as innocent as the child unborn, but surely, what sin hath God found out in me unrepented of, that he should lay such an affliction on me in my old age." To her unimaginable relief, the jury eventually found the old English lady not guilty but, appallingly, the judges directed the jurymen to reconsider their verdict. Under this outrageous pressure, they changed their finding to guilty and accordingly Rebecca was sentenced to death. Governor Phips immediately became the subject of pleas for mercy by Rebecca's family and in the light of these and of testimonies to her good character from some citizens who had retained their sanity, Phips granted her a reprieve. The ensuing protests against this supposedly unjustified leniency were such that, displaying pusillanimity of character, he reneged on the reprieve, to his later and lasting regret. The mental torture Rebecca endured during this off/on/off/on again death sentence process is not easily imaginable. But finally doomed, she was taken by cart to Gallows Hill where she struggled for dying air 3,000 miles from where she had taken her first breath on the other side of the Atlantic Ocean.

'The Witch House', Salem: the home of Judge Jonathon Corwin, a chief judge in the infamous witch trial

Rebecca's sister, Mary, who was married to English-born Isaac Eastey, a farmer and barrel-maker, shared Rebecca's pious nature and when her trial came, she earnestly assured the judges of her equal innocence: "I never complied with Satan but prayed against him all my days. I have no compliance with Satan . . . I will say it, if it is my last time, I am clear of this sin". Her accusers would have none of it. One, sixteen-year-old Mercy Lewis, claimed that even in the courtroom Mary was still remotely-controlling her actions. Thus, when Mary clasped her hands together, Mercy replicated the gesture and claimed she was unable to un-stick her hands; and when Mary bowed her head, Mercy claimed she could feel her own neck breaking. Nevertheless, the judges appeared not entirely convinced of her guilt and sent Mary home. But the merciless Mercy was not a girl to give up easily and a few weeks later she claimed Mary was again afflicting her, and badly so. Her testimony was supported by other girls who alleged Mary was evilly afflicting them too. Consequently, the authorities dragged Mary from her bed at night, returned her to prison and, surprise, surprise, proceeded to find her guilty after all. As in the case of her sister Rebecca, Mary was soon literally carted-off to Gallows Hill, where she was hanged in company with seven others. Prominent citizen and preacher Cotton Mather, whom we have met elsewhere in these pages, denounced them as "eight firebrands of hell" and was an enthusiastic spectator at the executions. (Mather was a grandson of John Cotton, the famous Vicar of St. Botolph's Church in Boston, England, whose story is to be found in another chapter of this book, *The Pilgrim Fathers and the Original Boston*.)

Sarah, the third, (Salem-born) Towne sister, did not escape attention either and also languished in jail while her sisters were tried and executed, but was eventually set at liberty, in her case there seeming to be some persistent doubts. She was fortunate, for in all nineteen women and one man were put to death. Some of their accusers were eventually to regret what they had said and done; for example, twenty years later Anne Putnam specifically named the three Towne sisters as among those she had falsely and wickedly accused: "I should lie down in the dust and humble myself for having brought upon them and their families so sad a calamity". One is reminded of what have been described as the two saddest words in the English language: "Too late".

What of the one Salem man who was put to death? Giles Corey by name, he was a prosperous though uneducated 80-year-old farmer who had been born in Northampton, England. (It must be conceded that he cannot be regarded as without a stain on his character, for in 1676 he had so severely beaten one of his farmworkers, for allegedly stealing apples that the poor fellow died. Since the law permitted corporal punishment to be employed against servants, Corey was merely charged with using "unreasonable" force and fined.) When the Salem witches episode burst forth, his wife, Martha Corey, took the brave but dangerous step of challenging the "bewitched" girls' claims; they – and this cannot be thought of as a great surprise – immediately responded by accusing her of being a witch herself. When she was interrogated by a magistrate in their presence, the girls asserted they could see a yellow bird suckling on a witch's teat between her fingers and that a spectral version of her was endeavouring to strangle them there and then. The aforementioned Anne Putnam added for good measure that she had once looked out of the dining room window of her parents' house and seen husband Giles praying to the Devil. Naturally, this led to his being interrogated as well, and husband and wife alike were thrown into jail. When Giles's case was brought to court, two young sisters called Booth – whose imaginative abilities in other circumstances would surely have to be admired – testified that they had once seen him serve the Devil's sacrament of blood and bread to a coven of witches numbering at least fifty!

As it became clear to Corey that whatever he said or did, he would be found guilty of being a 'wizard', i.e. a male witch, he became immensely concerned for the future of his family. This was because, as a male, a guilty verdict would involve not only his execution but the seizure by the authorities of all his assets including his house, cottages and farm, thus depriving his daughters, sons-in-law and grandchildren of all that he and they had toiled for over decades. Faced with the prospect of their being homeless and penniless, he decided to take advantage – if that is the word – of a way out offered by a quirk of the law, though at terrible personal cost. In a nutshell, the quirk was the stipulation that if a person refused to plead – refused to say either 'guilty' or 'not guilty' – he must be pressed under ever-increasing weights until he either recanted his refusal or died. In the case of persons persisting until they perished, they could not be said technically to have been found guilty, and thus no assets could be confiscated. The courageous eighty-year-old Corey determined to take this dreadful course.

On Monday 19th September men of the village dug a grave-shaped pit in an open field next to Salem jail. Escorted by the Magistrates, official witnesses and maudlin sightseers, Corey was led to it and stripped of all his clothes. He was laid flat, face upward, on the floor of the pit and wooden boards placed over him. Six stout men then lifted heavy stones and lowered or threw them onto the boards, commencing the process of inflicting wracking pain on the octogenarian's body. But not a word or cry emerged from him, despite his being vilely abused and hectored to submit. After two interminable days and nights (during which he was granted nothing but three mouthfuls of bread and water, which he proved almost incapable of ingesting) he was again enjoined to plead innocent or guilty to the charge, the question being repeated three times. His chest crushed and struggling to get the words out, he simply pleaded, "More weight", so that his sufferings might be brought to an earlier end. More rocks were added and Sheriff Corwin indulged his taste for sadism by several times standing on top of them and observing Corey's bulging eyes. One witness, Robert Carey, later recorded: "In the pressing, Giles Corey's tongue was pressed out of his mouth; the Sheriff, with his cane, forced it in again". Eventually, the old man cried out "More weight" for the final time and, shortly before dying, found just enough breath to curse Sheriff Corwin and the entire town of Salem.

Poor Martha Corey was hanged three days after Giles expired. Her execution was not marked by any vicious doggerel of the type which shortly thereafter marked her husband's passing:

Giles Corey was a wizard strong, a stubborn wretch was he;

And fit was he to hang on high upon the locust tree.

So, when before the Magistrates for trial he did come,

He would no true confession make but was completely dumb.

"Giles Corey," said the Magistrate,

"What hast thou here to plead

To those who now accuse thy soul of crime and horrid deed?"

Giles Corey he said not a word, no single word spoke he.

"Giles Corey," said the Magistrate, "We'll press it out of thee".

They got them then a heavy beam, then laid it on his breast;

They loaded it with heavy stones

And hard upon him pressed.

"More weight," now said this wretched man.

"More weight!" again he cried;

And he did no confession make but wickedly he died.

Surely, though, we can detect in the primitive verse its author's sneaking admiration for Corey, most markedly in the abundantly-justified title which he (or possibly she) bestowed on it: *"The Man of Iron"*.

In conclusion, it may be asked – had those Norfolk-born sisters Rebecca and Mary Towne remained in their home town of Great Yarmouth, would they have escaped the fear of witchcraft accusations there? The answer is undoubtedly 'no', for at the time of their births the infamous Matthew Hopkins, the self-appointed 'Witchfinder-General', was masterminding the notorious campaign which resulted in the deaths of over 300 'witches', almost all of them in the East Anglia region, of which of course Great Yarmouth was a part. Indeed, by the standards set by Hopkins and his credulous adherents, and despite the tragedies which unfolded in the sisters' new home in the New World, the Witchfinders of Salem, infamous though they are, must almost be accounted amateurs . . .

NORFOLK

The First of America's First Ladies
(who survived by eating rats . . .)

The role of the 'First Lady' looms large in American national life, much as the consorts of the Kings and Queens of England have done for many a century. Though Martha Washington laid the first official claim to the title as wife of President George Washington, in social terms Martha had long before been beaten to the winning post by a young Englishwoman called Temperance Flowerdew. She assumed the role of America's first 'First Lady' when in 1618 her second husband, Sir George Yeardley, was appointed as the Royal Governor of Virginia, Britain's first colony in the New World. As consort of the King's representative, her status was unrivalled by any other woman in British North America.

Temperance was the daughter of Anthony Flowerdew of what was then the small village of Hethersett in Norfolk, England, and of his wife Martha, who hailed from Scottow, a hamlet in the same county. In 1609 Temperance married for the first time, to a man called Richard Barrow, and later that year the couple embarked for the New World aboard the *Falcon*, part of a convoy of ships bound for Jamestown. Two months or so into the voyage, the convoy encountered an horrendous storm and the flagship, the *Sea Venture*, was separated from the other vessels: it was feared that she had sunk with all hands. In fact, she had been blown far off course and shipwrecked on the coast of Bermuda, though her crew and passengers survived. Amongst them was a young lieutenant, George Yeardley, whom Temperance could not have then foreseen would become her second husband following Richard Barrow's early death. (The reader might also be interested to know that John Rolfe, who was to become the husband of Native American princess Pocahontas, was also aboard the *Sea Venture* and that Shakespeare was later in part drew on the vessel's fate for his play *The Tempest*.)

The Market Cross at Wymondham:
Temperance Flowerdew would have known this well as a child,
for she would often have accompanied her parents there
on market days from their nearby home in Hethersett

The *Falcoln,* battered but still afloat – Temperance and Richard probably rather battered too – limped into Jamestown eventually. The settlement's struggling residents were shocked to learn of the presumed loss of *Sea Venture,* for she was the vessel which had been transporting the great bulk of the supplies they so desperately needed. The new arrivals were equally shocked, in their case by the conditions they found ashore, especially the chronic shortage of food. Into this plight and worse, Temperance and her companions were themselves quickly plunged, for they had had the misfortune to arrive at the onset of the wretched winter known as Jamestown's 'Starving Time'. During this period conditions deteriorated to the point of famine. George Percy, Jamestown's chief citizen, wrote in his journal: "Now all of us at Jamestown, beginning to feel the prick of hunger, which no man can truly describe but which he hath tasted the bitterness thereof. A world of miseries ensued . . . and some, to satisfy their hunger, have robbed the store, for which I caused them to be executed. Then having fed upon horses and other beasts as long as they lasted, we were glad to make a shift with vermin, as dogs, cats, rats and mice. All was fish that came to net to satisfy cruel hunger, as to eat boots, shoes, or any other leather some could come by. And those being spent and devoured, some were forced to search the woods and to feed upon serpents and snakes and to dig the earth for wild and unknown roots, where many of our men were cut off and slain by the Indians. And now famine beginning to look ghastly and pale in every face that nothing was spared to maintain life and to do those things which seem incredible . . ." Only one in five of the colonists, including the new arrivals, was to survive this dreadful period. Temperance was one of them, which speaks volumes for her resilience and courage. How many times, with nothing but roasted rodent for dinner, must she have dearly wished she was back in her familiar village of Hethersett in Norfolk, properly fed, sheltered and warmed.

As can readily be imagined, there was much rejoicing amongst the little band of survivors in the spring of 1610, when against all odds the crew and passengers of the stricken *Sea Venture* belatedly but triumphantly themselves arrived in Jamestown, carried in two small vessels they had ingeniously constructed from *Sea Venture*'s wreckage. Now, at last, the settlement could and would turn the corner and gradually make the ascent to a more civilised and comfortable level of life.

Temperance's husband Richard was not to witness the improvement though, for he was one of those who had met their deaths in the Starving Time or a little after. Certainly Temperance had become a widow by 1617 at the latest, for in that year she re-married, her favours falling on George Yeardley, the young officer who had sailed with her in the convoy of 1609. Her choice was a wise one: Yeardley had done well in the New World and by now was the Deputy Governor of all Virginia, no small achievement. Shortly

141

after their wedding, Yeardley and his bride returned to England for an extended honeymoon. They based themselves in St. Albans in Hertfordshire with Yeardley's prosperous elder brother Ralph, whose house was at the sign of "the Artichoke" (possibly on the site of the present public house of that name at Croxley Green.)

A recipient of royal favour for his achievements as Deputy Governor, Yeardley, wife Temperance with him, was at some point invited to join King James I and his party at the famous horseraces at Newmarket in Suffolk. There the King knighted him and appointed him as Virginia's full Governor in succession to the then current Governor Sir Samuel Argall, whom Yeardley was ordered to arrest on his return! Argall, apparently, was deemed by King James to have been exceptionally repressive and not to have the colonists' best interests at heart.

Sir George Yeardley, as he now was, revelled in his new distinctions. A contemporary reported a week later that he had "set him[self] up so high he flaunts it up and down the streets in extraordinary braverie with fourteen or fifteen fair liveries [uniformed servants] after him". Certain we can be that Temperance was adorned and handmaided in equally extravagant style, for a man's wife was, of course, a symbol of himself.

Following Yeardley and Temperance's return to Virginia, the colony continued to grow and develop, the new gubernatorial couple contributing to the increase in its population by becoming the parents of three children. The family lived well, dwelling in style on the south side of the James River on an estate granted him by King James; Yeardley named it the Flowerdew Hundred in Temperance's honour. On these fertile acres Yeardley cultivated tobacco (shipped and sold to England), grew corn, and reared livestock. Amongst other things, he also built America's first windmill, at a cost of £120 in 1621. All in all, he became a very wealthy man and consequently Temperance was able to import luxury items – especially dresses and jewellery of the latest fashion – from the mother country as and when she desired. Organising and presiding at balls, banquets and other social events commensurate with her husband's pre-eminent status, Temperance made the Governor's Mansion the pinnacle of the young colony's social life. But there was a brutal side to existence in Virginia, too, for in the early hours of March 22nd 1622, in a carefully-orchestrated attack on the English invaders, the Powhatan 'Red Indians' wiped out twenty-five percent of the colonists, including six of the thirty or so people who lived on the Flowerdew Hundred. Though Yeardley, Temperance and the children survived the carnage, Temperance – not for the first time in her life – must have been dreadfully afraid.

In 1627, Yeardley died of natural causes but Temperance smartly retained her status as First Lady by deftly and rapidly marrying his successor, Governor Francis West, sadly only for herself to die nine months' later. However, until the very end, she remained the doyenne of early Virginian society, sought after as both hostess and honoured guest by all the leading members of the burgeoning colony, an exemplar of contented family life, a noted exponent of charity towards the poor, and an able consort to her husbands in the discharge of their duties. She was, indeed, "The First of America's First Ladies". The humble young woman from far-away Hethersett and survivor of the Starving Time had, in every sense of the word, come a very long way.

NORFOLK

President Abraham Lincoln's Ancestral Home

In 1637 a young apprentice weaver named Samuel Lincoln left, forever, his home village of Hingham in Norfolk, England to embark on a perilous journey to a new Hingham in Massachusetts. This event, seemingly of small consequence to the wider world, was in reality epoch-making, for it was to culminate in the election of Samuel's descendant Abraham Lincoln to the presidency of the United States. And in the pantheon of American presidents, Abraham Lincoln is, of course, universally acknowledged as one of the most illustrious – indeed, he contends with George Washington as *the* most illustrious. For was it not Abraham Lincoln who held the new nation together in the great crisis of the American Civil War, abolished slavery, and set the USA on the path to its place in the modern world? The saga is nowadays symbolised by the memorial bust of Abraham in old Hingham's Church of St. Andrew, the church in which his forebear Samuel was baptised and later worshipped. The memorial, presented in 1919, was the gift of Americans for whom old Hingham was, is, and no doubt always will be, a place of pilgrimage.

Samuel Lincoln was born in 1622 and baptised on 24th August that year. He was the son of smallholder Edward Lincoln and his wife Bridget. Bridget had been a resident of Hingham since birth, but as a child and young man Edward had lived with his parents at their home in nearby Swanton Morley. He had made his move to Hingham after falling out disastrously with *his* father (a man not at all short of money) when the latter made a will couched in terms which would bequeath Edward precisely nothing. We have no knowledge as to how on his arrival in Hingham the alienated Edward was able to acquire his smallholding, but we do know that he was never to succeed in doing much more than scrabble for a living. Consequently, he was unable to provide Samuel (and Samuel's many siblings) with more than the bare necessities of life. It is not surprising, therefore, that on attaining working age Samuel was promptly apprenticed – one less mouth to feed! – to Frances Lawes of Norwich, a weaver: a modest position indeed for the forebear of a President.

Samuel Lincoln's family home at Swanton Morley - the centre section of The Angel Inn

Significantly, by the time of Samuel's move to Norwich, his elder brothers Thomas and Daniel had already established themselves on the far side of the Atlantic, for they had been among the religiously-inspired group who had left old Hingham in 1633 to found the new Hingham in Massachusetts. This family connection to the New World probably led to discussions between Samuel and his master about opportunities for advancement there, for in 1637 Frances Laws announced that he, his wife Lydia and daughter Mary were about to take ship for the new Hingham themselves. Would Samuel like to go with them? Samuel *did* like, and so did a servant of

Lawes named Anne Smith. Thus it came about that on 8ᵗʰ April the little party embarked on the *John and Dorothy* of Ipswich and on 20ᵗʰ June landed at Boston, Massachusetts.

Within a few months of arrival in the New World Samuel either completed his apprenticeship or was released from it by agreement, for he moved to Salem (of witches' fame) and spent several months there before returning to the new Hingham, where he helped to build the Old Ship Church. There are some references to his continuing to work as a weaver but when in 1649 he bought a house and two acres of land the deeds described him as also being a mariner – an eclectic combination of pursuits. It's probably not co-incidental that at about the time he made his property purchase he also married, his favour falling on Martha Lyford, the daughter of the Reverend John Lyford of Berkshire in England and his wife Sarah. Samuel and Martha were to become the parents of eleven children, of whom the most significant, from history's point of view, was Mordecai, born in 1655, for he was the forebear of the famous Abraham. "A husky boy and full of energy", Mordecai became a blacksmith of considerable ability, for he went on to establish the first smelting furnace in New England and eventually became an iron-founder on a significant scale.

In stark contrast, Mordecai's direct descendant, Thomas Lincoln, one day to be the father of the President, was illiterate. Born in 1778, in his twenties Thomas took up residence in the wilds of Kentucky where he lived by the sweat of his brow. (His elder brother had inherited everything, Thomas nothing, when their father had been killed by a marauding 'Red Indian'). Thomas was a thrifty man, though, and managed to save enough money from carpentry and labouring to buy a small farm. In 1806 he married Nancy Hanks, a Virginian woman, and in 1809, in the family's one-room, dirt-floored, log cabin, Nancy gave birth to Abraham, the second of their three children.

Although Thomas Lincoln prospered to a degree in later life, existence at this time was hard and money short and in consequence Abraham received little in the way of formal education. But encouraged by his mother, who *had* benefitted from some schooling, the lad evinced a determination to educate himself and did so with success, mainly by devoting himself to reading whenever he had a spare moment. (He obtained his books from every conceivable source, begging, borrowing and, when he had a little money, even buying.) This frequently incurred Thomas's wrath and he did not hesitate to "slash" Abraham for being buried in books on occasions when he should have been completing chores. Neighbours, too, were to some degree suspicious about what one termed the young fellow's "reading, scribbling, writing, ciphering, writing Poetry, etc.", deeming this "laziness"! Moreover, if Abraham ever queried his father's views or corrected his version of a story, he received a literal slap in the face; and when Thomas sent him out to work for neighbouring farmers, Abraham was not permitted to keep a penny of his pay. Some have speculated that as a consequence the young Abraham began to feel he was little more than a slave, which may throw light on his later views. When his father lay dying, the adult Abraham refused to visit him, telling a relative, "Say to him [Thomas] that if we could meet now, it is doubtful that it would not be more painful than pleasant". He emphasised the point by refusing to pay for a headstone for the grave. By contrast, he loved his mother Nancy deeply, describing her as an "angel".

When the family moved to Illinois in 1831, Abraham struck out on his own, initially pursuing some fairly menial ways of earning a living. He moved up the ladder a little by buying a general store on credit but it did not prosper. The future president then became variously a postmaster in New Salem, a surveyor, and a captain in the Illinois Militia. He began to participate in politics and in 1834 was admitted to Illinois's House of Representatives as a Whig. (At the risk of over-simplification, it can be said that the fundamental stance of the American Whigs was one of opposition to tyranny and to this end they favoured the dominance of the Congress over the presidency. They also favoured modernisation and manufacturing.) Professionally, though, Abraham's over-arching ambition at this time was to become a lawyer. In typical fashion, he set about it by first reading and re-reading the four volumes of Blackstone's

Commentaries on the Laws of England (for English law was, of course, the bedrock of United States' law too.) In 1836 he was admitted to the Bar and soon established a powerful reputation. He also succeeded in advancing as a politician and graduated to the national House of Representatives. He then left politics for a while, acknowledging his unpopularity amongst Illinois voters for his opposition to the Mexican-American War of 1846-48, which had been initiated by the United States and was highly controversial even amongst its own citizens. The war was particularly opposed by the Whig party and by an alliance of anti-imperialists and anti-slavery campaigners, who perceived the conflict as an act of colonial expansion and aggression – this by a country born amidst the rhetoric of freedom and independence. Be that as it may, the ruling United States government succeeded in its aims and a vast swathe of Mexican territory, including Texas, was forcibly incorporated into the USA.

The Mexican-American war over, Abraham returned to politics in 1854, taking a prominent part in the establishment of the new Republican Party and from the start making plain his opposition to slavery. Over the next six years he grew ever more prominent on the national stage, culminating in 1860 in his nomination as the Republican Party's candidate for the Presidency. He succeeded handsomely, if not overwhelmingly, receiving 40% of the popular vote. But within a few weeks the newly-annointed President Lincoln, descendant of a humble apprentice from a land 3,500 miles away across the Atlantic, had to face a crisis of massive proportions – namely, in quick succession, the secession from the Union of South Carolina, Mississippi, Florida, Alabama, Georgia, Louisiana and Texas, soon followed by North Carolina, Tennessee and Arkansas – eleven states in all. These Southern states had followed a very different path over the years from their Northern and Western counterparts, the South developing itself primarily as an agrarian economy, relying heavily on black slaves, while the North had developed as much more of a manufacturing-based society.

The young nation thus began to tear itself apart and a war lasting four years and costing 600,000 lives ensued. President

Abraham Lincoln, hailed by the world, steered the Union to victory despite innumerable setbacks and so re-cemented the United States of America into one indivisible unit. No summary of the war is required here, for the story is one of the most extensively recorded and analysed in history. It will suffice to highlight two things for which the Hingham descendant will forever be remembered.

First, Lincoln's Emancipation Proclamation: "That on the first day of January one thousand eight hundred and sixty three, all persons held as slaves within any State . . . shall be then, thenceforward and forever free . . ."

Second, Lincoln's immortal Gettysburg Address of 1863, which followed the burial of Union soldiers who had fallen on the battlefield of that name, and of which this is an extract: "Four score and seven years ago our fathers brought forth on this continent a new nation, conceived in liberty, and dedicated to the proposition that all men are created equal . . . from these honoured dead [here at Gettysburg] we take increased devotion to the cause for which they gave the last full measure of devotion – that we here highly resolve that these dead shall not have died in vain – that this nation, under God, shall have a new birth of freedom – and that the government of the people, for the people, shall not perish from the earth." He added: "The world will take little note nor long remember what we say here." That part of his speech, and that part alone, has proved wonderfully, triumphantly and immortally mistaken.

But all was soon to end in tragedy, for on the evening of April 14th 1865, Lincoln was indulging in rare relaxation by attending a performance at Ford's Theatre in Washington D.C. He was accompanied by his wife, Mary. The play was the farce *Our American Cousin* by the English playwright Tom Taylor and featured a naïve young American's visit to England to claim his inheritance of the family estate, where, in particular, he encounters a brainless English nobleman called Lord Dundreary. Chuckling in common with the rest of the audience, the President was completely unaware of the existence of a twenty-eight year old man called John Wilkes Booth lurking nearby, armed with a Derringer revolver. Booth was American by birth but 100% English by blood. His parents were the well-known British Shakespearean actor Junius Brutus Booth and his mistress Mary Ann Holmes, who had emigrated together to Maryland in 1821. John Wilkes Booth grew up to be an avid supporter of the breakaway Southern States and a convinced believer in the institution of slavery. On the day prior to Lincoln's attendance at the theatre, Booth had witnessed him make a speech advocating freed slaves being granted the right to vote. For Booth this was the final straw and he was heard to swear it was the last speech Lincoln would ever make.

True to his word, at about 10.00pm Booth entered the theatre, slipped into the Presidential box and shot Lincoln in the back of the head. He then jumped from the box onto the stage where he shouted "Sic semper tyrannis', meaning "Thus always to tyrants" – surely the most erudite war cry ever uttered by an assassin and no doubt unintelligible to the vast majority of the shocked theatregoers. Avoiding attempts to intercept him, Booth fled the theatre to his getaway horse and galloped into Maryland. Eventually, he was located at a farm owned by the Garrett family. He was found in a barn with an accomplice (of whom Booth had several) and this accomplice, David Herold, quickly surrendered. Booth refused to do so, saying he preferred to fight. The surrounding soldiers responded by setting fire to the barn, thus forcing Booth out. He was immediately shot and fatally wounded by Sergeant Boston Corbett, an immigrant Englishman born in London. Booth died a few hours' later. In his diary, which he had carried with him, he had written of Lincoln's death: "Our country owed all her troubles to him, and God simply made me the instrument of his punishment". So speaks the disease of religious and racial fanaticism throughout the ages.

Go now to the church in old Hingham. Contemplate the memorial to Abraham and touch the font where the Lincoln who started it all, Samuel, was baptised on August 24th 1622.

The author's wife in St. Andrew's church, Hingham,
holding the first American flag – the Grand Union Flag –
by the memorial to Abraham Lincoln

NORFOLK

General Benjamin Lincoln:
You win some, you lose some . . .

With the exception of Abraham Lincoln himself, the Lincoln family member who achieved the highest position in public life was a man whom history seems largely to have forgotten: Major General Benjamin Lincoln, no less a person than George Washington's second-in-command for a period during the American Revolution and, after independence, the new nation's first Secretary of War.

Benjamin's parents were Benjamin Lincoln senior and his wife Elizabeth (nee Thaxter). As was the case with Abraham, Benjamin senior's ancestors had come from old Hingham in Norfolk, England [7] and established themselves in the new Hingham when it was part of the Massachusetts Bay Colony. However, Benjamin was considerably more fortunate in his early life than Abraham was to be in the following century, in that his parents enjoyed a modest level of prosperity. He was born in 1733 and in his early years worked on the family farm. At the age of 21 he obtained his first official post as Hingham's town constable. Shortly afterwards, in 1755, at a time when as part of the Seven Years' War the Colonists and the British Army were fighting the French and Indians in North America, he went on to join 3rd Regiment of the Suffolk County Militia.

He obtained little if any experience of front-line battle during his service but in the early days of the Revolution went on to prove himself valuable to the rebel forces by organising supplies. In January 1776 he was promoted to the rank of Major General. Thereafter he was to play a significant part in hostilities, sometimes

---

7   For fuller, reliable information about Abraham and Benjamin Lincoln's ancestry, the reader is referred to "The Ancestry of Abraham Lincoln" by Henry Lee & J.R. Hutchinson (Houghton Mifflin Co. Boston and New York 1909) and the Lincoln Genealogical Tables compiled by Ellen Smith and others. Certain websites are *not* reliable.

with success (for example, in the British defeat at Saratoga at the hands of rebel forces commanded, ironically, by British-born, former British Army officer General Horatio Gates). But, it is fair to say, Benjamin Lincoln was more often to find that success eluded him. In his first action of consequence, the Battle of Bound Brook, he was roundly defeated by General Cornwallis and was lucky not to have become a British captive. Later, at the battle of Bemis Heights, an American victory, Lincoln was caught up in a skirmish with a British company and his right ankle was shattered by a Redcoat's musket ball. Eventually, he returned to Hingham to recuperate but his right leg was left permanently two inches shorter than the left. Back in action in 1778, Lincoln participated in the unsuccessful French-led siege of Savannah, Georgia and was forced to retreat to Charleston. Charleston was soon surrounded by the British and after a short siege Lincoln humiliatingly surrendered his troops, more the 5,000 of them, to Lieutenant General Sir Henry Clinton. It was the biggest American surrender of the war. This time Lincoln did fall captive to the British but in November 1780 they released him as part of a prisoner-exchange agreement.

General Benjamin Lincoln's house
in the new Hingham in Massachusetts

The freed Benjamin's moment of glory was to come a year or so later, when, restored to service, he participated as Washington's second-in-command in the crucial Franco-American victory at Yorktown, Virginia – historically accepted as the turning point of the war. There, a British force of 8,000 was surrounded by a roughly 50/50 French and American force of 16,000. The British held out against the larger force for three weeks and, crucially, were prevented from evacuating themselves by sea by the arrival of a very large French fleet under the command of Admiral de Grasse. The British commander, Lord Cornwallis, had to reluctantly conclude that de Grasse's coup made his position hopeless. Accordingly, Cornwallis surrendered and the magnitude of his surrender was signified by a British drum and fife band playing, in a commendably sporting gesture, *'The World Turned Upside Down'*. Washington, too, made a sporting gesture, not to the British but to Benjamin as his own second-in-command, by deputing him to formally accept Cornwallis's sword – a comfort to Benjamin for having had to surrender his own sword to Cornwallis after the American defeat at Charleston. It must be remarked here that Washington clearly valued Benjamin, for reasons that are not perhaps entirely clear in the light of Benjamin's mixed military record, part of which comprised his reputation for nodding-off to sleep at unpredictable moments. (Indeed, after one defeat of a Franco-American force, Benjamin was blamed by the French for having dozed-off at a crucial moment. One of Benjamin's own officers maintained, however, that "General Lincoln was 'never found asleep when it was necessary for him to be awake'"! Nowadays Benjamin would probably have been diagnosed as suffering from sleep apnoea).

Perhaps the biggest irony of the Cornwallis/Lincoln clashes was the fact that Lord Cornwallis's ancestral home at Culford in Suffolk, England, was but a few miles distant from the original Hingham, from which, only a couple of lifespans previously, the Lincolns had departed in order to make new lives in America. Thus does history twist and turn, and underline the ingenuity of men of even the same native blood in finding reasons to butcher one another.

Benjamin Lincoln concluded his career with the distinction (as noted earlier) of being the new nation's first Secretary of War. He eventually retired to his home in the new Hingham, where he died in 1810. His house can be visited to this day.

NORFOLK

The Priest Who Wrecked His own Church and Fled to America

In the early 21ˢᵗ century Hingham in Norfolk, England, gives little sign of being troubled by any deep divisions, but in the early 1600s it was riven by religious strife. It was also a substantially smaller settlement then, and the nation as a whole much less populous too. (In fact, the total number of inhabitants of England and Wales was little more than five million, as opposed to about 60 million in 2017). Thus the Norfolk of those days displayed far fewer signs of human habitation and Hingham must have felt isolated and remote. It was from this little village, however – as described in the chapters about President Abraham Lincoln and General Benjamin Lincoln – that a number of members of the Lincoln family emigrated to America in the 1630s. Here, however, we shall recount the story of the village's vicar, the Reverend Samuel Peck, a charismatic Puritan who fled to the new Hingham in Massachusetts when the old Hingham became too hot to hold him.

The story unfolds in 1605 when the 25-year-old Peck was appointed as the parish's rector. Peck was a native of Beccles in Suffolk and a graduate of Magdalen College, Cambridge, where he became a Bachelor of Arts in 1559 and a Master of Arts in 1603. He was a zealous preacher, scathing of ritual, of Church ornamentation and of what he considered to be lingering Roman Catholic practices and superstitions still disfiguring Anglican worship. In short, he sought a 'purified' church, from which he found some of his persuasion amongst his new parishioners, and it is even possible that they had lobbied for his appointment. Even so, he was not without his detractors in the village, for one local opponent described him as a man of "violent and schismatical spirit", though this was countered by an admirer who maintained he was "a godly, loving and peaceable minister". One thing is certain: for over 30 years Peck was a dominant and powerful figure – probably *the* most dominant and powerful figure – in the parish.

Robert Peck's church – St. Andrew's, Hingham

Be all that as it may, from his earliest days in the village Peck zealously expounded Puritan doctrine, both from the pulpit of the parish church of St. Andrew's and in villagers' homes. For many years he escaped ecclesiastical punishment for displaying these heretical tendencies only because his bishop, John Jegan of Norwich, was himself a man of Puritan learnings and happy to place Peck under his protection. However, things became less easy for Peck when Bishop Jegan was replaced by Bishop Samuel Harsnet in 1619. Soon afterwards, Harsnet charged Peck with a major offence, namely that he had "infected the parish with strange opinions as not to kneel when they [the parishioners] come to church, that the name of Jesus is no more than a common name and that it is superstitious to bow at the name of Jesus". But, somehow or other, Peck survived Harsnet's assault and soldiered on. But in 1633, in common with others of his persuasion, Peck faced yet further difficulties, triggered by the promotion of William Laud to the most important post in the Church hierarchy, the Archbishopric of Canterbury. Laud was an autocratic man and determined to take a hard line with everybody and everything that departed from Church of England norms. Many people believed that he covertly favoured Roman Catholicism – in common, it was said, with King Charles II, the man who had appointed him. In short, Laud as an individual was an enemy of Puritans and the views he expounded were anathema to them.

One of Laud's early stipulations was that each and every church in the country including, of course, St. Andrew's at Hingham, should establish or re-establish an elevated High Altar on the east wall of the chancel, to replace the simple table placed facing south under the chancel arch which since the Reformation had been in use as the focal point of church services. Laud further ruled that the High Altar be protected by a rail "so this with pillars that dogs may not get in". This latter point may seem, and indeed be, entirely reasonable, for churches in those days were frequently used as social and business meeting places and dogs were often free to roam around inside – hardly conducive to a spirit of calm holiness. However, Laud's motive ran much deeper: what he really wanted to do was to re-emphasise the role of the parish priest as the unchallenged arbiter of correct theological thinking, and to mark that distinction by physically separating and elevating the priest and the altar from the congregation. The congregation's role, in Laud's view, was simply to listen carefully to what the priest said and to accept and obey without question. In contrast, Puritanism held that each worshipper should be largely free to study the Bible for himself or herself, thus receiving God's Word direct and without manipulative intervention from a misleading or mischievous third party. (Peck, of course, would not have considered himself ever to have been misleading or mischievous!) Thus, Laud's enforced physical changes to the country's churches became a great point of controversy and bitterness and emblematic of irreconcilable theological differences.

In 1636, three years after Laud's edict, the simmering and all-devouring theological dispute manifested itself violently in Hingham when, on Peck's instructions, a large number of his parishioners broke into St. Andrew's Church – their own place of worship – and destroyed the new altar rails, which they then threw into a pit. They trumped this by lowering the High Altar so that it was a foot blow the church floor, thereby demonstrating their contempt for it as a lingering symbol of Roman Catholicism.

At the time of these events the Bishop of Norwich was another hard-line man called Matthew Wren, a stout ally of Laud. Wren was appalled by what he perceived as this outrage at Hingham. Holding Peck personally responsible, Wren charged him with "contumacious disobedience to the orders and ceremonies of the church". The implacable Peck and his principal associates refused to recant or obey, and Wren retaliated by excommunicating them, levying heavy fines and expelling Peck from his post as rector. Faced by this disaster, Peck and his followers concluded they had little alternative but to leave England and make a fresh start in the New World, just as the Pilgrim Fathers and others – including not a few from Hingham – had done already. Thus, after a period of raising funds and disposing of assets (often in forced sales at half their value), in June 1638 the Reverend Peck and 132 other Hingham men, women and children, including members of the Lincoln family, boarded the little 35-ton ship *Diligent* at Ipswich in the neighbouring country of Suffolk and set sail for the new Hingham in Massachusetts, which had been established by some of their friends and neighbours in 1633. After the usual difficult and protracted voyage in cramped and unhealthy conditions, the weary but excited party put themselves ashore near Boston.

The Hingham emigrants, in preparing for their journey, had at least had the advantage of advice arising from the experience of the Hingham settlers who had preceded them. Helpful advice was, in fact, often sent back to the Old World. For example, the Reverend Francis Higgins, the first minister at Salem, compiled a checklist. "Before you come", he wrote, "be careful to be strongly instructed what things are fittest to bring with you for your more comfortable passage at sea, as also for your husbandry occasions when you come to the land. For when you are once parted with England you shall meete neither markets nor fayres to buy what you want. Therefore be sure to furnish yourselves with things fitting to be had before you come: as meale for bread, malte for drinke, woollen and linen cloath, and leather for shoes and all manner of carpenters tools, and a great deale of iron and steel to make nails, and locks for houses, and furniture for ploughs and carts, and glasse for windows, and many other things which were better for you to think of there than to want them here".

What was life like in the new Hingham? The historian of the settlement, John D. Long, writing in the 19th century, found from his study of the records that, unsurprisingly, it was "toned by the ecclesiastical atmosphere which the clergy gave to [it]". However, he also found that, once the earliest difficulties had been overcome, "men and women engaged in the ordinary activities of life, cultivating the farms, ploughing the seas, trading with foreign lands and among themselves, engaging in near and remote fisheries, maintaining the school, the train-band [primitive military force], the church, holding their town meetings". He assessed the people of the new Hingham to be "not without humour but not innocent of a modicum of quarrel and greed either". On the whole it seems the new Hinghamites had a neighbourly spirit, the accounts they left redolent with "everyday details of farm and home, of domestic affairs, of straying cattle and swine, of runaway apprentices and scolding wives, of barter with the Indians, of whippings and stocks and fines for all sorts of naughtiness, of [disputes over] boundaries, [law] suits, of debt and legal processes and probate, of elections and petty offices civil and military, and now and then the alarum of war and the inevitable assessment of taxes". Thus, through the efforts of the people, the new Hingham was eventually to prosper, despite the differences of opinion between the early Puritan faction and the more disparate groups of English people who in due course also settled there.

But here we must note that even as Peck and his band of 130 or so departed from old Hingham in 1638, the long-running struggle for power between King Charles I and Parliament was reaching crisis point. The King's policies were unpopular, taxation was a massive bone of contention, and religious schism lurked beneath everything, for the King was rightly suspected of lingering Roman Catholic leanings. His most fervent antagonists, the by-now very strong Puritan bloc in Parliament and their many followers nationwide, were to the fore in all these matters and by 1641 the outlook was bleak; indeed, there were already forebodings in some quarters that an armed conflict might break out. At this point, Peck's old parishioners in Norfolk sent a message pleading with him to return from the New World to guide them through what they anticipated were going to be very difficult times in the Old. Peck consented and was back in the English Hingham by the time the King raised his battle standard at Nottingham in August 1642, thereby marking the start of the series of English Civil Wars – some of the very bloodiest the world has known. Amongst all the ensuing years of fighting, Peck performed his religious duties unofficially but faithfully and in 1645 was triumphantly and officially re-appointed as old Hingham's Rector.

The Puritans, of course, under the leadership of Oliver Cromwell, emerged victorious nationwide in 1651, and the by now elderly Robert Peck no doubt wept tears of joy. He retained the Rectorship of old Hingham until 1656 when he died in harness of natural causes, blissfully unaware that only a few years hence the Puritans and all their works would themselves be overthrown and the monarchy re-instated.

This remarkable and turbulent man, Robert Peck, still lies buried, somewhere, in the peaceful graveyard of his own original Church. Wander round it, and his church, and meditate. And, if you can, visit the new Hingham in Massachusetts, whose citizens still recall their links to the old Hingham and send civic delegations across the Atlantic to pay homage to their town's origins in the Old World.

NORFOLK

Norwich and Benjamin Franklin, "The First American"

Benjamin Franklin is renowned as a founding father of the United States of America, and indeed is frequently described as "the first American". For the sixteen crucial years of 1757 to 1775 he was the principal diplomatic intermediary between the colonists and the British Government; then, after the two sides came to blows, he went on to become a draftsman of the Declaration of Independence, a principal architect of the new American nation, and its first-ever overseas ambassador. He was many other things, too – writer, printer, newspaper proprietor, statesman, diplomat, scientist, philosopher and inventor. In short, he was a polymath – a man of remarkable expertise in many spheres. He was a dab hand at devising pithy quotations, too: if you've ever heard the aphorism, "Nothing in this life is certain except death and taxes", or if you've been advised by an admonishing elder that "Early to bed, early to rise, makes a man healthy, wealthy and wise", you have been the beneficiary of some of his thoughts.

His multifarious talents and his inclination towards public service ultimately combined to create a dazzling mix of scientific and civic 'firsts' to add to his portfolio of political achievements. He invented the lightning conductor and bifocal glasses. He was the first person to determine that the common cold was passed from human to human by indoor air and the first to use the words 'positive' and 'negative' in relation to electricity. He established America's first learned society (the American Philosophical Society), America's first public hospital (Pennsylvania Hospital), America's first circulating library (The Library Company of Philadelphia), America's first volunteer fire department (The Union Fire Company), and America's first mutual insurance company (The Philadelphia Contributorship). Neither were day-to-day domestic matters beneath his notice, for he also invented a highly-effective stove (the 'Franklin Stove') and was the first person to propose Daylight Savings Time. Moreover, he wrote extensively and memorably, penning everything from *Advice to a Friend on Choosing a Mistress*, through *Experiments and Observations on Electricity* and the wildly-popular *Poor Richard's Almanac*, to *The Drinker's Dictionary* and *The Way to Wealth* – an eclectic assortment indeed.

Norwich Guildhall, already more than 200 years old when it was familiar to Franklin's Norfolk forebear as the civic heart of his home city

Benjamin was a man of 100% English blood. His mother, Abiah, was the daughter of Peter Foulger of Norwich in Norfolk and his wife Mary, and his father was Josiah Franklin of Ecton, a small village in Northamptonshire.

The aforesaid Peter, a Baptist, left Norwich for Massachusetts in 1635 at the age of twenty-eight, and it was on his voyage to the New World that he met fellow-emigrant fifteen-year-old Mary. For whatever reason, the couple's relationship took nearly a decade to

163

blossom into marriage but marry they eventually did. The groom, it would seem, was a man of some education for in his new home of Watertown in Massachusetts and later in Martha's Vineyard he paid his way by teaching and land-surveying. He had, too, the distinction of being hired by the Governor to preach Christianity to the Native Americans, for which purpose he learned the local tribal language. Later he became a clerk in the Law Courts. All in all, he displayed in embryo something of the multi-faceted abilities later to manifest themselves so dramatically in Benjamin.

Mary, by contrast, scraped a living as an indentured servant and in order to marry her in 1644 Peter had to buy her out of the indentureship for the sum of £20. This, said Peter, was "the best appropriation of money [I] ever made". However, it was not until 1667 – in other words, not until after twenty-three years of marriage – that Mary gave birth to their daughter Abiah, Benjamin's mother-to-be. Fortunately, all went well with the birth, despite the fact that Mary had reached the advanced age for childbirth of 47. We know little else about this mother of such a notable son but she has achieved a degree of literary immortality, for she is mentioned by name as a real character in Herman Melville's fictional *Moby Dick*. Melville depicts her as having "something better than royal blood" by virtue of her being "kith and kin to noble Benjamin . . ."

Benjamin's Ecton-born father, Josiah Franklin, came into the world in 1657. Josiah's own father was the village blacksmith. Josiah himself became a fabric dyer and married a fellow-villager, Ann Child. When the couple emigrated to Massachusetts in 1682 and started their new lives in Boston, he perforce took up the trade of tallow chandler and soap boiler – Boston, apparently, having no call for any more fabric dyers. Sadly, Anne was soon to die in childbirth, and so there came about Josiah Franklin's second marriage, to the aforementioned Abiah. The wedding ceremony took place in Boston's Old South Church in 1689 and the Franklin couple's youngest son, the one-day-to-be-illustrious Benjamin, was born in 1706. To say the least, Benjamin was never to be a lonely child, for he was one of ten boys and seven girls!

The London residence of Benjamin Franklin at
36 Craven Street, now a museum devoted to his life

Josiah and Abiah Franklin were responsible parents, keen that their offspring should do well. However, despite its soon becoming apparent that Benjamin was an exceptionally bright boy, Josiah's limited income and the enormous demands on it precluded Benjamin from receiving anything more than two years' elementary schooling. Consequently, at the age of ten, formal education abandoned, Benjamin perforce took up full-time work in his fecund father's candle and soap shop. Undaunted by this premature immersion in the world of work the young lad, then and for many years' afterwards, manifested an iron determination to complete his education by his own efforts. Devouring books from every available source, he taught himself arithmetic, grammar, history and philosophy and at the same time made himself familiar with diverse matters technical and scientific. Crucially, he also nourished his capacity for self-expression by composing essays, and soon became adept at writing lucidly, compellingly and with insight – and amusingly, too.

After two years working in the candle and soap shop, Benjamin changed course by taking up an apprenticeship with his elder brother James, the proprietor of a small printing works. Four years into the apprenticeship, when Benjamin was sixteen, James founded a weekly newspaper called *The New England Courant*. Benjamin was keen to contribute to it but feared that his brother would reject his efforts for, he recorded, James was "harsh and tyrannical". Benjamin was thus driven to submit essays and commentary anonymously under the pen-name of "Mrs. Dogwood", a purported widow who "offered homespun musings on everything from fashion and marriage to women's rights and religion". So popular were these that 'Mrs. Dogwoood' soon received numerous proposals of marriage!

When James learned that "Mrs Dogwood" was in reality Benjamin, the brothers' relationship deteriorated still further and in 1723, at the age of seventeen, Benjamin left Boston for Philadelphia. In Philadelphia he gained employment as a printer but his ambition to establish a printing works of his own was stymied by a lack of capital. The bright but impoverished Benjamin's difficulty was eventually brought to the notice of no less a personage than the Royal Governor of Pennsylvania and Delaware, Scotsman Sir William Keith, who arranged for him to go to London to purchase equipment. Vitally, Sir William promised to supply his supposed protégé with letters of credit and introductions to influential persons. On arrival in London, Benjamin found he had been cruelly duped, there being no letters of credit and no introductions. A friend called James Ralph told him "there was not the least probability that [the Governor] had written any letters for me; that no one who knew him had the smallest dependence on him; and he laughed at the notion of the Governor's giving me a letter of credit, having, as he said, no credit to give. On my expressing some concern about what I should do, he advised me to endeavour getting some employment in the way of my business. 'Among the printers here', said he, you will improve yourself and when you return to America you will be set up to greater advantage'." Franklin must have been devastated. As he was to record in his autobiography, ". . . what shall we think of a Governor's playing such pitiful tricks and imposing so grossly on a poor ignorant boy!" But later he expressed himself in amazingly forgiving terms: "He [Governor Keith] wished to please everybody; and having little to give, he gave expectations. He was otherwise an ingenious, sensible man, a pretty good writer, and a good governor for the people, though not for [the colony's ruling elite] whose instructions he sometimes disregarded. Several of our best laws were of his planning and passed during his administration."

Having little alternative, Franklin took his friend's advice and stayed in London, polishing his skills as a printer at Palmer's, a famous printing house in Bartholomew Close. Later he transferred his employment to "Watt's, near Lincoln's Inn, a still greater printing house". Throughout, he continued to read avidly and also published his first pamphlet, *A Dissertation on Liberty and Necessity, Pleasure and Pain*. The pamphlet did not go un-noticed and led to Franklin's first foray into London's intellectual world. There he made a number of notable acquaintances, amongst them the highly-renowned Sir Hans Sloane, the physicist, naturalist and collector. But Benjamin sought pleasure, too, "spending a good deal of my earnings in going to plays and other places of amusement". Amatory dalliance also received a fair share of his attention, and he attempted to seduce his friend James Ralph's mistress. She rebuffed him and the friendship of the two men unsurprisingly foundered.

After eighteen months in London, Benjamin decided the time had come to return to America. Despite the initial disappointment brought about by Governor Keith's duplicity, Benjamin, though little richer, had greatly enjoyed himself in the Old World, learned much and "had picked up some very ingenious acquaintances, whose conversation was of great advantage to me".

Returning to Philadelphia in 1726, Benjamin initially made a living by bookkeeping and shopkeeping. However, he remained keen to exploit his London-honed printing skills, and after short-term employment by an English-born Philadelphian printer by the name of Samuel Keimer, succeeded in opening his own print shop. His mastery of his profession and reputation for reliability soon led to his obtaining a contract to print Government books, pamphlets and other official publications, and in 1730 he was appointed as the Official Printer for Pennsylvania. With cash earned from the publication of an admired pamphlet advocating an increase in the money supply, he bought from Keimer a newspaper called *The Pennsylvanian Gazette* and soon turned it into the most widely read in all the British colonies. From this point on, he went from strength to strength, notably by writing and publishing the immensely popular *Poor Richard's Almanac*, comprising weather forecasts, astronomical data, practical household hints, puzzles and other amusements, together with maxims of a memorable nature, e.g. "Fish and visitors smell in three days". (It must be admitted that not a few of these witticisms were 'borrowed' from the British nobleman and wit, Lord Halifax.) In course of time, Benjamin diversified into real estate and other businesses and became a very prosperous man. His eye for the fair sex continued to twinkle, too, and in 1730 he took as his common law wife an old flame called Deborah Reed.

By 1748 Benjamin was one of the richest men in Pennsylvania and he deputed a partner to look after his business interests to enable him to spend more time pursuing other enthusiasms, particularly his fascination with electricity. For example, he conducted a famous experiment with a kite during a thunderstorm in which he demonstrated that lightning was itself a form of electricity, and found in England a publisher for his book, *Experiments and Observations on Electricity*. He also began to involve himself in political affairs and secured election to the Philadelphia City Council and the Pennsylvania Assembly. During the French and Indian War he went so far as to propose (at this point without the slightest idea of independence in his mind) that the thirteen colonies create a unified government to strengthen their defensive capabilities but, ahead of his time, he was unable to harness enough support.

Benjamin was by now a man who inspired great public confidence and in 1757, at the age of fifty-one, he was appointed by the Pennsylvania Assembly to serve as the colony's agent in England, later adding Georgia, New Jersey and Massachusetts to his portfolio. He was to remain in England for most of the next twenty years, revelling in the intellectual and scientific opportunities it offered, its theatres, its literary salons and the conversation of its learned men. He regarded himself as a loyal Englishman and took satisfaction in his pure British blood, factors which manifested themselves in a love for England and his retention of innumerable friends there until the day of his death. But, and it was a massive 'but', he gradually became to wonder if it would not be better for the colonies to manage their own affairs. This was partly inspired by his dislike of the corruption he perceived in British political and royal circles. In any event, things came to a head when the British Parliament passed the Stamp Act in 1765, which imposed the first direct duty on the colonists and led to enormous opposition. Benjamin's status in Britain was by now such that he was asked to appear before Parliament to give its members the benefit of his views on the subject. This he did, and the Stamp Act was rapidly repealed. With this, Franklin emerged as the leading spokesman in Britain for American interests.

But tensions between the colonies and the Mother Country continued, and for Benjamin personally what proved to be an unhealable estrangement with Britain occurred in 1773 when there fell into his hands some letters written by Thomas Hutchinson, the Royal Governor of Massachusetts. In them Hutchinson called for "an abridgement of what are called English liberties" in America. The appalled Benjamin leaked the letters and there was an enormous outcry in the colonies and amongst the colonists' many friends in Britain. Naturally, the London Government was mightily displeased and called Benjamin to appear before the Privy Council, which thoroughly lambasted him. No doubt deeply hurt, he reluctantly now gave up any real hope of conciliation between the mother and daughter countries and started to work actively for independence. He published, more in sorrow than in anger, a satirical essay portraying what he perceived as Britain's follies, *Rules by Which a Great Empire May Be Reduced to a Small One*, and this received wide acclaim.

At a personal level, these political differences between Britain and its American colonies brought about a never-to-be-healed rift between Benjamin and a personality not hitherto introduced into this account, his illegitimate son, William Franklin, who had been born in 1730 or thereabouts. Though we do not know the identity of William's birth mother, William had been reared by Benjamin and his common law wife Deborah with love and care and as if both of them (not Benjamin only) were his natural parents. When Benjamin had come to England as Pennsylvania's Agent in 1757, he had brought William with him, the first of several visits, long and short, William was to make here. A personable and good-looking young man, he had settled easily into English society, studied law here and was called to the English Bar. In England, Benjamin continued to develop confidence in his talented and much-loved son's abilities and judgement, so much so that in 1763 he used his influence with the British Prime Minister, the Earl of Bute, to secure William's appointment as Royal Governor of New Jersey. However, in profound contradistinction to Benjamin, William was to forever remain a devoted British subject, performing the duties of royal governorship loyally to the end. Following imprisonment by the rebels – his father's allies! – when the Revolution finally succeeded, he took refuge in Britain and was to remain here until his death, father and son never reconciled – an irony of history and above all, a family tragedy.

To return to Benjamin: he took ship back to Philadelphia in 1775 and was unanimously chosen by the Pennsylvanian Assembly as their delegate to the Continental Congress, the body which managed the colonists' war effort and moved the putative nation step-by-step to independence. He was appointed to the committee of five which drafted the Declaration of Independence and was one of the most distinguished of its signatories at the ceremony famously held on 4th July 1776. At the signing, in response to a remark that "We must all hang together," Benjamin riposted "Yes, we must all hang together or most assuredly we shall all hang separately". Later that year, he was appointed as ambassador to France and in 1778 he negotiated the Treaty of Alliance which, crucial to the colonists' ultimate success, brought France, their former enemy, into the war on the American side. He also succeeded in securing large loans which kept the rebels' military campaign afloat. (We must surely here concede that in doing these things Benjamin – the man who declared "Honesty is the best policy" – displayed more than a touch of that form of hypocrisy which masquerades as 'realpolitik'.)

In France, Benjamin's charm and intelligence, his wit, his simple backwoodsman's dress, did much to foster his great popularity there. And, though he spoke French but stumblingly, he was a particular favourite with the ladies with whom, even in his seventies, he did not cease to flirt. He returned to America for the final time in 1783 after playing a major role in that year's signing of the Treaty of Paris, which brought the war between Britain and the nascent United States to an end. Once back on the western side of the Atlantic, he became President of the Council of Pennsylvania, served as a delegate to the Constitutional Convention and wrote one of the last of his pamphlets, in which he condemned the slavery which he passionately believed disfigured a new country ostensibly dedicated to Liberty. At about the same time as Benjamin returned to America, son William crossed the Atlantic in the reverse direction to take up residence in England, where, as mentioned earlier, he remained until his death, a literal and metaphorical gap of 3,500 miles separating the conflicting loyalties of father and son.

Benjamin Franklin, that man of pure English blood who became "the first American", died aged 84, on 17th April 1790, his funeral attended by a vast crowd of admirers. His life on this earth was at an end but, as the Independence Hall Association of Philadelphia has expressed it, "his electric personality still lights the world".

NORFOLK & LINCOLNSHIRE

The Propagandist-in-Chief
Who Named the New Nation
"The United States of America"

Every successful revolutionary movement must have a propaganda department and for the rebellious colonists of the American War of Independence that department essentially consisted of just one man: Tom Paine of Norfolk in England. But that one man's output has seldom, if ever, been bettered in terms of power and effectiveness. The second U.S. president, John Adams, said of Paine: "Without the author of *Common Sense*, the sword of Washington would have been raised in vain." *Common Sense*, published at the start of the seminal year of 1776, was effectively the Bible-cum-handbook of the American Revolution. It represented only a small part of Paine's American revolutionary writings but was to become – and remains to this day – the best known of them; and, proportionate to population, it is the best-selling title in American history. Hugely seditious and inflammatory (as the British government saw it), *Common Sense* was crafted in compelling language and provided high-octane fuel for the motor of the rebellion.

Tom Paine was, as noted, an Englishman, born in Thetford, Norfolk in 1737, the son of Joseph Paine and his wife Frances (the daughter of Thomas Cocke, a lawyer and Thetford's Town Clerk). Joseph is often stated to have been a stay-maker, i.e. a maker of women's corsets; in fact, it is equally possible that the stays in question were 'stays' or 'stay ropes' used on sailing ships. The site of Paine's birthplace and childhood home is now occupied by the Thomas Paine Hotel but his schoolroom, a few hundred yards to the south, remains unchanged to this day. He studied there for five years, from age seven to age twelve, at which point he became his father's apprentice. At age sixteen, having mastered the stay-maker's art, and inspired by the romantic maritime yarns he had been told by one of his schoolmasters, he left home for the greatly more adventurous life of seaman aboard a privateer, privateers being semi-official pirate vessels licensed by the British Government to prey on the maritime fleets of unfriendly countries. (His first posting was to the *Terrible*, commanded by Captain Death, who was assisted by Lieutenant Devil and Mr. Ghost, the ship's surgeon!)

Thomas Paine's schoolroom at Thetford Grammar School,
virtually unchanged since when he studied there

Paine maintained this adventurous seaborne life for six years before opting to return to a more mundane existence ashore, where he set

173

up a small stay-making business of his own in Kent and married a girl called Mary Lambert who, sadly, was soon to die in childbirth. In 1761 he returned to Thetford, having secured employment there as an excise officer, i.e. a tax collector, for which on the face of it he seems to have been unqualified, but no doubt his father-in-law's connections helped. He left his Thetford post in 1764 for duty in Lincolnshire, first at Grantham and then at Alford (where his office was in the Windmill Hotel in the Market Place), and later at Lewes in Sussex. We have a description of how Paine appeared during his time in Lewes, left to us by a friend, Thomas Rickman. Paine was, apparently, about five feet ten inches in height, broad-shouldered and athletic, his eyes "full, brilliant and singularly piercing" with the "muse of fire" in them. Smartly attired, he "wore his hair cued with side curls and powdered, and looked altogether like a gentleman of the old French school". He was a prominent member of a local debating club, the Headstrong Club, where, the Dictionary of National Biography tells us, he developed a reputation as "an obstinate haranguer".

This impressive-looking if fiery individual was to remain in the excise service until 1774 except for a period following his dismissal for a disciplinary offence in the mid-1760s, though he contrived to obtain reinstatement after two years. It must be said that this re-instatement is more than a little surprising, for Paine's record as an excise officer was dismal, involving episodes of dereliction of duty, claims to have inspected goods he hadn't, absences without leave, lying, and inflaming fellow officers to agitate for improved pay and conditions. This latter, trade union-like activity – at a time when trade unions were illegal – witnessed the publication of his first pamphlet, *The Case of the Officers of Excise*. The outcome of all this was, of course, entirely predictable: the Excise Commissioners dispensed with his services finally and irrevocably in 1774. They were additionally and severely displeased that in his private capacity he had contracted many debts, which he was totally unable to repay.

USAAF B17 bomber in East Anglia and
the memorial plaque on the site of Paine's birthplace
(now the Thomas Paine Hotel, Thetford),
dedicated by USAAF airmen

At about the same time, Paine separated from his second wife, the widow of a friend – the marriage lasted only three years – and workless and indigent, he had no alternative but to sell whatever remained of his possessions to avoid debtor's prison. Amidst this unpromising circumstance, a friend introduced him to Benjamin Franklin (see the chapter *Norwich and Benjamin Franklin, the 'First American'*), an event which was to change Paine's life, for he took up Franklin's suggestion that he emigrate to British America. Barely surviving the voyage to Philadelphia because of an outbreak of typhoid aboard ship, he arrived just a handful of months before the crucial outbreak of violence at Lexington between Massachusetts Militiamen and a British Army contingent sent to destroy a weapons depot at Concord.

Paine immediately decided to support the rebels, not only from intellectual and philosophical conviction that this was the right thing to do but because, to use an English expression, he was always instinctively "agin [against] the government", whoever or whatever the "government" might be – the national government, some other country's government, his employers, social or group leaderships or even, in the end, hitherto admired figures in movements to which he had previously given his support. Paine soon placed his enormously powerful pen at the disposal of the rebellious colonists and, in January 1776, published his aforementioned 96-page pamphlet *Common Sense*, emphasising that it was "written by an Englishman". In cogent, colourful and stirring language, it advanced comprehensive arguments for the rejection of colonial rule. It sold out almost immediately and had to be reprinted time and again. In short, *Common Sense* became the rebellious colonists' holy book. He followed this later in the year with *The American Crisis*, which contains one of his most memorable calls to arms:

> *"These are the times that try men's souls: the summer soldier and the sunshine patriot will, in this crisis, shrink from the service of their country; but he that stands it now, deserves the thanks of man and woman. Tyranny, like Hell, is not easily conquered; yet we have this consolation with us, that the harder the conflict, the more glorious the triumph. What we obtain too cheap, we esteem too lightly: it is dearness only that gives every thing its value. Heaven knows how to put a proper price upon its goods; and it would be strange indeed if so celestial an article as freedom should not be highly rated."*

He kept up his output of propaganda throughout the war years, much of it in a series of essays published in the Pennsylvania Journal. He boosted rebel morale in dark times by "puffing American successes in small skirmishes and supporting the decisions of [General Nathaniel] Greene and [General George] Washington despite their frequent military blunders". Towards the end of the war he accepted a salary from Congress to write in favour of the taxes it was by now imposing – something of an irony in that aversion to taxes lay at the heart of the revolution! At the conclusion of hostilties he was rewarded with £500 in cash by Pennsylvania and $3,000 dollars by Congress, and New York granted him ownership of a farm at New Rochelle which had been confiscated from an oppressed Loyalist.

Always happier in demolishing a status quo rather than establishing something new, Paine took no part in the creation of the new republic and diverted himself by producing designs for iron bridges. He returned to the Old World in 1787 and visited his 91-year-old mother in Thetford (arranging for her to receive a pension of nine shillings a week), dividing his time thereafter between Britain and France. One wonders what kind of reception he initially received in his home country, bearing in mind that a substantial number of Britons had supported American independence: if he had kept his head down, all might have been well but he did not. Consequently, he was eventually forced to flee to avoid a charge of sedition brought against him by the British Government.

Tom Paine's statue, Thetford, presented by the
Thomas Paine Society of the USA

However, with the advent of the French Revolution, Paine's revolutionary instincts were soon to come to the fore again. In 1791 his hugely influential *Rights of Man* was published – a handbook for this second great rebellion. By way of thanks, Paine was granted French citizenship and elected to the National Convention as the member for Calais but he became alarmed by the revolutionaries' virtually-uncontrolled and sadistic violence. In particular, Paine opposed the execution of King Louis XVI and consequently he himself was incarcerated in the Luxembourg Prison in Paris. He emerged with his life and freedom thanks only to the intercession of the American Minister to France, Thomas Jefferson. Still unbowed, he proceeded to give his support to the emergent Napoleon Bonaparte and enthusiastically and traitorously (not to mention naively) endorsed the idea of a French invasion of England, advocating the construction of a 1,000 vessel fleet for the purpose. However, as Napoleon moved towards dictatorship, Paine withdrew his backing, excoriating Napoleon as "the completest charlatan that ever existed". Disenchanted, in 1802 Paine returned to New Rochelle to live on his farm.

Paine's final years were characterised by poverty, poor health and alcoholism and, despite his long and invaluable support for the American revolutionaries, he was to a great degree now cold-shouldered by them. In part, this was because his anti-Christian and atheistic views had never gone down well and in part because he advocated the extension of the right to vote to men who did not own property – a concept as shocking to the largely well-to-do rulers of the new and avowedly democratic United States as it was to their opposite numbers in Britain. Nevertheless, it was – as he said himself – "no small thing" to have played a part in two world-shattering revolutions, and this must have profoundly comforted him as he approached his death in 1809. No doubt he also took more than a little pride in the fact that in late June 1776 he had been the first person to publicly call for the new nation to be named the "United States of America", the term being duly enshrined in the Declaration of Independence signed a few days later.

In 1964 the Thomas Paine Society of the U.S.A. erected a statue in Thomas Paine's honour in his birthplace of Thetford. On it are inscribed what are perhaps the noblest words he ever wrote: *"My country is the world and my religion is to do good."* The bronze Thomas Paine now perpetually gazes upon the 15th century Bell Inn, which as a schoolboy and young man he would have walked past almost every day. Behind him stand Thetford Town Council's offices, once the site of a royal hunting lodge favoured by King James I. If Paine's spirit is aware of that fact, he is no doubt more than a little pleased that in death, as in life, his back remains turned on royalty forever.

SUFFOLK

Otley Hall:
The Birthplace of British America

Fabulous Otley Hall

Go to exquisite 15th century Otley Hall (which lies a mile or two from the Suffolk hamlet from which it takes its name). Stroll through its beautiful gardens. Enter the house on open days and linger in its exquisite rooms. Do these things and you will be at the very epicentre of the English colonisation of North America. For Otley Hall was the ancestral home of the Gosnold family and their scion Bartholomew. Bartholomew was the man who advocated and planned the establishment of Jamestown in Virginia, the first permanent and successful English settlement in what – two or three lifespans later – was to become the United States of America.

Bartholomew was born in 1571 and spent most of his childhood in Otley Hall, where he shared a tutor with his brothers, sisters and cousins. And what a place it was for these young people to enjoy when released from the confinement of lessons. The gardens would have echoed to the sound of their frolics and laughter. Later, as a young married man Bartholomew lived in nearby Bury St. Edmunds but returned to the Hall many on many occasions to spend time with his relatives – in front of a roaring fire in winter or over a convivial meal at the end of a sunny summer's day – often talking about his ambition to establish a colony in the New World.

The family's original intention had to fit Bartholomew for life as an educated country gentleman, for after completing his education at Otley Hall he was entered as an undergraduate at Jesus College, Cambridge. In 1590 or thereabouts he went on to study law at the Inns of Court in London – always a useful asset for a man with prospects of land and money. More importantly, he began to evolve a passionate interest in the sea, with all its exciting prospects of discovery and adventure. Some say he was influenced in this direction by Otley neighbour Richard Hakluyt, author of the renowned work *Principal Navigations*. Others hold the view that his enthusiasm was sparked by his marriage in 1595 to Mary Golding of Bury St. Edmunds (in which highly attractive town they settled down), for her family possessed numerous nautical connections. There was money in Mary's family, too, and links to high personages, most significantly to Francis Bacon, Keeper of the King's Seal.

In 1597 Bartholomew and Mary's daughter Martha was born and she was baptised in St. James' Church, now St. Edmundsbury Cathedral. The year was also marked by Bartholomew's first seafaring expedition, to the Azores with Queen Elizabeth I's favourite, the Earl of Essex. For twelve months or so thereafter Bartholomew continued his alliance with the noble Earl by assisting him in his capacity as a privateer preying on Spanish shipping – a privateer being in effect a legal pirate licensed by Her Majesty to prey on the vessels of unfriendly nations. Privateering was a paying game, Essex was good at it, and the young man from Otley's share of the loot very quickly amounted to a small fortune.

The great Hall at Otley, with its magnificent fireplace:
Bartholomew Gosnold would have sat here talking about
America and dreaming his American dreams

It was at about this time that Bartholomew began to focus his attention on the establishment of a colony in Virginia. His patron Essex was no longer in any position to help him fulfil the ambition, for in a brainstorm Essex had gone on to stupidly launch a hopelessly-doomed rebellion against Elizabeth, in the light of which the monarch had little difficulty in deciding that her wisest course of action was to separate his head from the rest of his body. However, one of Essex's accomplices in the misbegotten venture had been another earl, Southampton, who was fortunate enough to have been condemned only to the lesser punishment of incarceration in the Tower of London. Bartholomew had enjoyed a long friendship with Southampton and the latter, despite his imprisonment, had the will and the ability, even from his prison cell, to back Bartholomew financially in a plan to fulfil his American dream. The adventurous young Suffolk man, having also at his disposal his recently-acquired privateering cash, was thus able to establish himself as captain of his own ship, the *Concord*. She was a small bark, 39 feet long at the keel and 17½ feet broad – little more than a matchstick to be tossed by the Atlantic waves. He gathered about him sailors and migrants numbered in the low thirties, of whom twenty were to found the settlement. This sounds a remarkably small number to be left to fend for themselves on an alien shore three thousand miles from home, but that is what they willingly signed-up to do.

The churchyard in Bury St. Edmunds,
where Martha of Martha's Vineyard lies at rest

All preparations having been made by the Spring of 1602, Bartholomew and his fellow adventurers set off on their transatlantic voyage. They sailed via the Canary Islands in accordance with the old sailors' adage, "go south until your butter melts and then turn right". They made landfall in May at Cape Elizabeth, near what is nowadays Portland, Maine. There Bartholomew and his companions commenced to explore the coast in detail with a view to selecting a site that would have the desired characteristics for successful settlement. Deciding to turn south, he soon came across a cape projecting into the Atlantic which was hallmarked by the great profusion of cod in its surrounding waters. Appropriately, if unimaginatively, Bartholomew gave it the name 'Cape Cod'. A little south of the Cape he encountered some islands, the largest of which was characterised by an abundance of wild grapes – "Vines in more plenty than in France". In salute to this and – of much greater significance – in memory of his first-born child who had died as a small infant, he named the island 'Martha's Vineyard'. Martha had been laid to rest by Bartholomew and his wife in the great churchyard between the Cathedral and St. Mary's Church in Bury St. Edmunds and rests there still, though the exact location of her grave is now lost; but you may wander through the churchyard today and in your mind's eye perceive the grieving parents committing their little girl to the earth.

Bartholomew now espied another small island (today called Cuttyhunk) and named it Elizabeth Island in honour of the Queen. This spot, Bartholomew believed, showed promise, so he gave orders for the party to land. They built a small fort but soon found themselves surrounded by hostile Native Americans who vastly outnumbered them. Moreover, they soon realised that the quantity and nature of the supplies they had brought across the Atlantic would be inadequate to support them until they reached the point of basic self-sufficiency. So, after gathering cargo of cedarwood and sassafras (a type of deciduous tree), Bartholomew and his men reluctantly departed for the long voyage home. Disappointed though he was, as *Concord* departed Cuttyhunk Bartholomew vowed to himself that, one day, he would return to America, on a bigger scale and better resourced. The vow that was to dominate the remainder of his all-too-short life.

Back in England, for several years Bartholomew again laboured to put an expedition together. He lobbied his wife's cousin, the very rich London merchant Sir Thomas Smythe, and Smythe and Richard Hakluyt (he who lived near Otley) submitted to King James I (who by now had succeeded Elizabeth) a proposal to establish a colony with royal blessing. Involved, too, was

Edward Maria Wingfield, Bartholomew's distant cousin. There was universal delight when in 1606 King James received the proposal with enthusiasm and granted a royal charter creating the Virginia Company. Now with royal backing and access to another potent supply of money, a three-ship fleet was put together, comprising the *Sarah Constant*, the *Discovery* and the *Godspeed*, the latter being commanded by Bartholomew who was also appointed vice-admiral of the small fleet. The Admiral was Captain Christopher Newport of Harwich in Essex, probably selected for this sea-faring responsibility in preference to Gosnold by those with most money invested in the project because of his greater age – he was in his mid-forties – and his long experience. He had been a privateer for nearly twenty years and in 1592 had captured and brought back to London the Portuguese treasure ship *Madre de Dios*, which carried in her the greatest plunder of the century.

The new fleet with its 104 male settlers and 55 crewmen suffered an inauspicious start, trapped by storms at the mouth of the Thames for six weeks. Eventually the winds dropped and the trio of vessels was at last able to make progress. After calling in at the Azores en route, the colonists arrived in April at Chesapeake Bay. There Bartholomew and his senior associates selected for settlement a spot they named Jamestown in honour of the King. The first, enforced, priority for the newly-arrived Englishmen became the construction of a rudimentary fort, for though they had been welcomed by some of the Powhatan tribe who inhabited the area – and, indeed, been offered food and entertainment by them – another faction had subjected the newcomers to volleys of arrows and had had to be driven off by gunfire. The man the colonists had relied on to mastermind the fort's construction was a brawny young carpenter from Lincolnshire by the name of William Laxon [8] (or Laxton). He succeeded in erecting it with commendable speed but immediately after its completion the undeterred Native Americans subjected it to a determined assault. Though once again successful in repulsing their attackers, the colonists realised that a

---

8 For more about William Laxon, please see
   The Man Who Built America's First Houses

considerably more sophisticated defensive works would be required if long-term security was to be assured. Once again, therefore, Laxon was called upon to utilise his carpentry and supervisory skills and a considerably larger, triangular fort was erected. This boasted bulwarks at each corner, each of them furnished with four or five pieces of artillery. Inside the triangle, three public buildings were constructed – a church, a storehouse and a guardhouse. George Percy, one of the pioneers, proudly recorded: "The fifteenth day of June we had built and finished our fort . . . We had made ourselves sufficiently strong for these savages". Almost immediately, the new fort proved its indispensability, for the Englishmen had to fight-off a third attack by four hundred of their formidable 'Red Indian' foes, whose land they had invaded. Bartholomew played a major part in resisting the assault, scattering many of the attackers by firing on them with *Godspeed*'s heavy cannon.

However, the Native Americans had as their ally in resisting the English invaders something immensely more powerful than bows and arrows and spears and courage – Nature itself, specifically, deadly infection. In this respect the Englishmen's choice of location, though superficially attractive, had been an unwise one. The land was low-lying and mosquito-infested, and summer temperatures were very high. Thus, malaria, dysentery and swamp fever soon began to take their toll and most of the 104 settlers died from these and other causes. Amongst them was Bartholomew Gosnold himself, who breathed his last in August, only three months or so after arrival. Sadly, he had had but a brief period in which to experience life in the historic little settlement which represented the culmination of his life's work – and even those were much marred by difficulties. But we can be grateful that his historic achievement was recognised even at the time by his fellow pioneers for, as historians Warner Gookin and Phillip Barbour have said, they made their farewell to the man from Otley Hall "with proper instinct for the man they had lost, honourably buried [him], shattering the silence of the primeval forest with the crackle of volleys of small shot and the thunder of the discharge of all the ordnance in Jamestown Fort".

186

Though Bartholomew had reached his end, Jamestown, of course, had not. The acorn from which the oak of modern America grew, it clung courageously to life and in 1616 became the capital of the colony of Virginia, a status it retained for 83 years. Today it is a place of pilgrimage.

Wonderfully, the site of Bartholomew's burial place has in recent times been identified through forensic detective work by the Jamestown Rediscovery Project and a simple memorial erected: it faces the ocean which brought Bartholomew to his final resting place 3,000 miles distant from the land from which he had sprung. Whether we are able to personally pay our respects at his grave or not, we who have come after can testify to something he was never to know: that in his short life, through his implacable ambition of establishing his countrymen from the Old World in the land of the New, he has earned the right to be remembered as the prime mover in establishing what is today the United States of America.

No small epitaph, that.

SUFFOLK and NORFOLK

When the British Burned the White House

On September 27th 1814 British Major General Robert Ross had the pleasure of compiling a report to the Prime Minister, the Earl of Liverpool, at 10 Downing Street, London, which opened with these words: "I have the honour to communicate to your lordship that on the night of the 24th instant, after defeating the army of the United States that day, the troops under my command entered and took possession of the city of Washington." As Ross went on to recount, consequent on the Americans' defeat and their abandonment of the city, the British Army had set ablaze the whole of governmental Washington, including the President's mansion. Completely gutted internally, it proved impossible for the mansion's subsequent restorers to remove the disfiguring burn marks from its exterior walls. Their only recourse was to camouflage them by painting them white; thus, the seat of American presidential power was to become famously known as the White House. Amongst the troops responsible for the memorable torching were the predecessors of today's Royal Anglian Regiment, the 44th Regiment of Foot, founded by the Duke of Norfolk in 1689. The regimental headquarters are today in Bury St. Edmunds in the neighbouring county of Suffolk.

Here is the background: in 1812 a war lasting two-and-a-half years broke out when the United States of America declared war on Britain. In essence, the conflict was linked to Britain's simultaneous struggle against Napoleonic France, for in pursuit of victory the British had imposed an embargo on trade with the French and enforced a shipping blockade on neutral nations including the U.S.A. The Americans contended this was illegal under international law but the British rejected the claim and continued to intercept American ships. The British also pursued a vigorous policy of boarding American vessels to search for British-born sailors for impressment into the Royal Navy, for the need for sailors for the British fleet in this time of war was acute and American vessels were a tempting source of supply. (It is estimated that 9,000 British-born but naturalised-American sailors were crewing American ships at the time). An incident which particularly rankled with the USA had occurred in 1807 when the British warship HMS Leopard pursued, attacked and boarded the American frigate USS Chesapeake. American pride was humbled by the failure of the Chesapeake to fire more than one shot before surrendering. Such was the humiliation, a clamour for war and revenge arose amongst the American people. However, President Thomas Jefferson calmly and successfully sought a diplomatic settlement of the incident and so, for the time being, all-out hostilities were averted. Ill-will and confrontations nevertheless continued and eventually, in 1812, President James Madison and Congress did indeed declare war on the former Mother Country.

Gibraltar Barracks, Bury St. Edmunds,
Regimental Headquarters of the Royal Anglian Regiment,
successors to the 44th Foot

A principal component of the ensuing American strategy was their decision to invade Canada, a British territory the Americans lusted after and believed was ripe for the taking. It is this aspect of the war that is directly relevant to the story of the White House, for not only did the British bloodily repulse the invasion of Canada but followed up their successful defence by smashing their way down into the United States, one purpose being to punish the Americans by destroying Washington, their new seat of government.

In command of the British attack on Washington was the aforementioned Major General Ross, whose force of 4,500 included sailors and marines under Admiral Sir George Cockburn and, notably, the Duke of Norfolk's 44th Regiment of Foot. The 44th were formidable troops, skilled and toughened by their recent participation in the Napoleonic wars. The British were opposed by about 9,000 Americans under the command of Brigadier General William Winder. Winder's men, however, were of variable quality and included many militiamen, and Winder further weakened their chances by making few defensive preparations.

In the stifling heat of late August, in the hottest summer within living memory, Admiral Cockburn's sailors and marines advanced up the Patuxent River, driving back American Commodore Joshua Barney's gunboats and forcing the American to scuttle his fleet. Ross's troops simultaneously made their way to Bladensburg and its strategically-placed bridge over the eastern branch of the Potomac River (the Anacostia). Bladensburg was the key to any successful defence of Washington, and both sides knew it.

The Americans were confident of their ability to resist, however, so much so that President Madison and almost all of his Cabinet, accompanied by their principal aides, rode out from Washington to Bladensburg, eager to witness what they anticipated would be a resounding repulse for the British. They were to be sorely disappointed: failing to gain inspiration even from President Madison's presence, the American forces gave way catastrophically in the face of determined British attacks and the survivors, along with their President, his Government colleagues and General

Winder, were soon streaming back in chaos. So precipitate was the Americans' flight that the retreat became known to both sides as "the Bladensburg Races". The 44th Foot played a leading part in the British victory in the "Races" and in the follow-up move on Washington. In recognition the Regiment was awarded the battle honour, "Bladensburg", thereafter to be proudly displayed on the Regimental Colours.

Re-enactment the 44th Regiment of Foot at Bladensburg

In Washington, reports of the disaster having already filtered through, American officials set about destroying files and papers and evacuating government buildings. Soon, they were to witness American soldiers fleeing through Washington's streets, adding to the sense of panic and despair. At the President's Mansion an elaborate victory dinner had been prepared for him and his colleagues and fine wines awaited joyful decanting. But egad! – to use an English word of the era – the food, the wines and the splendid place-settings had to be left in the kitchen or on the dining tables as the mansion was rapidly evacuated. One person who famously kept her head in the chaos was Mrs. Madison, who had remained behind to prepare the celebration. Coolly, she made certain that a precious portrait of George Washington was removed to a safe place to prevent its falling into the hands of the enemy. She told her sister, "If I could have [had] a cannon at every window; but, alas! those who should have placed them there fled . . . my whole heart mourns for my country." But, like the great bulk of Washingtonians, Mrs Madison had no choice but to escape with her entourage, fleeing west along Pennsylvania Avenue. Shortly thereafter, the City of Washington was abandoned to the British.

At eight o' clock in the evening General Ross established a camp just short of Washington's boundary. Important buildings could still be perceived in the gently fading light and so the British resolved to make their way into the city's heart without delay. Admiral Cockburn, accompanied by a bodyguard of 150 men, went in first by way of Maryland Avenue. A few hardy Washingtonians – about ten per cent – remained hidden in their homes, cautiously observing events. One described a "British Army that looked like flames of fire, all red coats and the stocks of their guns painted with red vermilion". One or two exceptionally resilient folk went so far as to fire some shots, killing a corporal. The British immediately responded by setting ablaze the buildings from which the shots had come.

The British then moved on to the Capitol, designed by the English architect William Thornton and perfected by a fellow Englishman, Henry Latrobe. (Thornton was a son of a Lancashire family with a sugar plantation in the British West Indies, though he had been repatriated to Britain as a small child and lived there until emigrating to the newly-created USA in his late twenties. Latrobe came from Pudsey in Yorkshire.) The young nation's new seat of government was not quite completed – it awaited its dome and portico – but the great building was in all other respects finished and had been beautifully decorated and furnished. The British forced the doors, admired what they found – "grandeur and magnificence little suited to republican simplicity" recorded one officer – and then set about the task of burning the great building, together with everything within it. The task was supervised by one of Admiral Cockburn's officers, a man called George Pratt who was a specialist in explosives and fire-making materials. Pratt and his team gathered together in strategic locations in the building vast piles of furniture and timbering, fortified the lot with explosives extracted from Congreve rockets (an early form of artillery weapon), laid fuses and retired to a safe distance. As he departed, one Royal Navy man glanced back at the clock over the Presidential Chair: "It was lighted up as the clock told the hour of ten".

The gutted Capitol after burning by the British

After watching for a while the results of their efforts, the British made their way along Pennsylvania Avenue to the President's Mansion, which, as we have seen, had been entirely abandoned. After weeks of marching and fighting the British found the magnificent presidential residence to be an amazing reminder of comfort and civilisation. Even better, the smell of the hot food suffused the spacious dining room and, wrote one officer later, "a large store of super-excellent Madeira and other costly wines stood cooling in ice in one corner". Another officer dressed up for dinner by helping himself to a fresh shirt of "snowy clean linen . . . belonging to no less a person that the chief magistrate [i.e. the President] of the United

States". After dining superbly and drinking toasts to "the health of the Prince Regent and success to his Majesty's arms by sea and land", the British set about the fire-raising task for which they had come. General Ross personally supervised the setting of a bonfire in Mrs. Madison's drawing room, interrupted only by a messenger from the French ambassador pleading for his own official residence to be spared. Chivalrously, Ross consented.

The huge piles of combustible materials which had been prepared were set alight by blazing torches thrown through the windows. Soon the flames engulfed the massive building and reddened the night sky as the British stood and gazed. Then, once again, soldiers, sailors and marines headed west on Pennsylvania Avenue, their next target being the offices of the newspaper the National Intelligencer, which was edited by yet another English-born Washington resident, Joseph Gales. Gales and his paper were well-known for their enthusiastic support for the war and, for some reason, had long taken particular delight in abusing Admiral Cockburn up hill and down dale. Now it was Cockburn's turn to take revenge and, once more, preparations were made to create a massive fire. However, two distressed Washingtonian ladies whose houses were close by and who feared the flames would spread to their homes pleaded with Cockburn to think again. Like Ross, Cockburn chose the path of chivalry – surely thus giving the lie to at least some of Gales' calumnies – and instead ordered the building's contents of every description, including of course the printing presses, to be destroyed. (Down to "the last letter C" of the stock of typeface" instructed Cockburn, so that Gales would never be able to print the name Cockburn again!) Finally, ropes were attached to the building's brick piers by sea-shanty singing naval bluejackets who hauled away until the entire edifice collapsed in heaps of rubble.

Next on the British hit list was the Patent Office, the Superintendent of which was the aforementioned Englishman, William Thornton, architect of the Capitol. Though many papers had been safely removed, due to shortage of time and manpower it had been impossible to cart away the large quantities of working models, prototypes and other novel machinery stored on the premises. Thornton begged the officer in charge to spare them and the building, speaking of the loss of knowledge to mankind. Major Waters, the officer assigned to the task, was an educated man sympathetic to Thornton's view and gave way to the pleas of his fellow Englishman, though no doubt he had to seek higher authority to his act of restraint.

The White House, gutted after being put to the flames by the British

It is impracticable in a short space to give an account of everything the British destroyed, but the list also included the Treasury Building, the Library of Congress, the War Office and the American Navy Yard (such of it as had not been set ablaze already by American sailors before they abandoned it). Perhaps the most spectacular display of pyrotechnics was the blowing-up of the great Arsenal at Greenleaf Point, which caused an earthquake-like tremor to run through the city and which wounded a number of British troops unwise enough to have remained too close for the purpose of admiring their handiwork.

Amongst all this destruction of *public* property, however, the British generally were amazingly scrupulous in respecting *private* property (in stark contrast to the Americans in their failed foray into Canada). The White House Historical Association of the USA tells us: "The most significant case of the British enforcement of the rule against wanton looting involved a soldier armed with a musket who robbed residents close to the charred skeleton of the President's Mansion. The first victim was Scots-descended John Macleod, proprietor of the Washington Hotel on Pennsylvania Avenue. After threatening to set fire to the building, the robber moved to the home of a second victim as a neighbour [who must have had confidence in British officers' ability and willingness to enforce discipline!] sped to British headquarters on Capitol Hill to sound the alarm. Two British officers galloped down Pennsylvania Avenue and entered the house of a third victim as he was being robbed. What happened next was witnessed by a Washingtonian. One of the young officers shouted, 'You villain! You have turned thief and are disgracing your country!' The thief denied doing anything wrong but he was contradicted by Macleod, the hotelier. Infuriated, the officer clenched his fist and punched the soldier so hard that his hat fell off. It was found to contain silk shawls and other valuables. When he saw this the officer whacked the thief with the butt of his pistol and threatened to shoot him on the spot unless he immediately set off for British headquarters. He was put on his stolen horse and escorted up to Capitol Hill. On the way he tried to escape but his luck had run out. He was paraded at headquarters and then shot dead. Two other British thieves caught by their own men were given one hundred lashes." (The Historical Association goes on to remind us that, in contrast to the British, many Washingtonians themselves became looters.)

Suffice to say that by the following day, when the British, their job done, retraced their steps to Bladensburg and over the bridge, every building and facility of importance to the United States Government lay a burnt and gutted wreck. Of course, the government infrastructure was eventually rebuilt and repaired but at enormous cost to the notoriously reluctant American taxpayer. (Ah, those British – always causing Americans to pay taxes!) The victorious British commander, General Ross, was not to survive to enjoy his triumph for long, however, for barely a month later he was shot dead by an American sniper at the Battle of Baltimore.

SUFFOLK

The Man Who Was Given Virginia as a Gift

Arlington Cemetery, Virginia is the most famous burial ground in the United States, the sacred resting place of thousands of American servicemen and women from all branches of the nation's armed forces. Adjoining it is the almost equally-famous Arlington House, built by the adopted son of President George Washington. Tradition asserts that both the burial ground and the house take their name directly from a long-dead English nobleman, the 1st Earl of Arlington of Euston Hall in the English county of Suffolk. That is questionable [9], but indirectly they most certainly did, for in 1673 the Earl and a fellow 'nob', Lord Culpeper, were granted proprietary rights to the *whole* of Virginia – a little matter of over 6,000,000 acres! Arlington (for simplicity we shall him that throughout, though he was not awarded the title until 1665) was granted his slice of pie by virtue of being a favourite and right hand man of King Charles II. Certain it is that he performed an eclectic variety of essential services for his royal master, amongst them fighting in the English Civil War, serving as his Secretary of State and – not least! – procuring and assisting in the management of the many royal mistresses . . .

Arlington was born in 1618, the son of Sir John Bennet of Dawley in Middlesex and of Dorothy, daughter of Sir John Crofts of Little Saxham which, like Euston, is in Suffolk and lies a dozen or so miles north of Euston as the crow flies. Arlington was educated at Westminster School in London and at Oxford University, at the latter institution gaining a reputation as something of a poet. Shortly after he left Oxford the English Civil War broke out and, as already mentioned, he took up arms for the King. In an encounter

---

9 The reader is referred to *The Arlington Connection* by Warren Clardy of the Arlington (Virginia) Historical Society

with Parliamentarian troops – 'Roundheads' – at Andover in 1644, he sustained a wound to the bridge of his nose which scarred it badly for life, causing him to camouflage it for evermore with a sinister black plaster. (A contemporary wrote: "This remarkable plaster so well-suited his mysterious looks that it seemed an addition to his gravity and self-sufficiency.")

When King Charles II and his brother James, Duke of York, fled to the Continent after the royal drubbing at the Battle of Worcester in 1651, Arlington loyally followed them and was appointed as James's secretary. On the restoration of the monarchy in 1660, King Charles poached Arlington's services for himself and appointed him Keeper of the Privy Purse. The Keeper was the official who looked after the monarch's personal finances – a post of pivotal importance to the high-spending, high-living and woman-chasing Charles. On a personal level, King Charles was much taken by his new 'money man' and so Arlington became a great favourite. When in 1662 he was appointed to the aforesaid Secretaryship of State he achieved the ultimate in Royal recognition – membership of the King's personal and secretive political clique, the famous or infamous 'Cabal'. Indeed, he was one of those who gave the initial letter of his name to the very word in its modern sense – an acronym for **C**lifford, **A**rlington, **B**uckingham, **A**shley, **L**auderdale.

Arlington's link with Virginia came about in 1673 when the King granted him and Culpeper the aforementioned proprietorship – beneficial ownership – of the entire colony for a period of 30 years. The terms of the grant were later toned-down a little in the face of fierce opposition from existing settlers but nevertheless Arlington and Culpeper continued to be the recipients of the lucrative stream of semi-feudal rents and taxes which flowed steadily back to this side of the Atlantic. Arlington, though more than happy to spend the Virginians' money, seems however to have been remarkably uncurious about the land and people that produced it, for never once did he visit his domains or, as far as we know, even express the slightest interest in doing so. It can be said that he was the very definition of an 'absentee landlord'.

Euston Hall, Suffolk

Not a little of the cash with which the Virginians reluctantly filled Arlington's coffers he spent on improvements to Euston Hall and Estate (he had acquired them in 1666 and re-built the Hall shortly afterwards) and on entertaining his benefactor, the King. This he did on a wondrous scale and on numerous occasions. The famous diarist Sir John Evelyn wrote of one visit: "Came all the great men from Newmarket and other parts both of Suffolk and Norfolk, to make their court [to the King], the whole house filled from one end to the other with lords, ladies and gallants; there was such a furnished table as I had seldom seen, nor anything more splendid and free, so that for fifteen days there were entertained at least 200 people, and half as many horses, besides servants and guards, at infinite expense." Arlington, Evelyn affirmed, was the ultimate exponent of "the fine art of entertaining, which he understood and loved better than any man in England'.

The "infinite expense" of royal entertainment to which Evelyn referred turned out to be the canniest of bloodline investments, for the King's son Henry FitzRoy and Arlington's daughter Isabella later became husband and wife. Fitzroy, illegitimate though he was, had from birth been proudly and publicly acknowledged by the King; his mother was the beautiful, captivating and Catholic Lady Barbara Castlemaine, who contended with former orange-seller Nell Gwynne as the best-known of King Charles's mistresses. (On one occasion, an anti-Catholic mob intimidatingly rocked a coach under the mistaken impression that Lady Castlemaine was aboard. "Catholic whore!" they yelled. Their jeers turned to cheers when to their surprise the feisty Nell stuck her head out of the carriage window: "No, no!" she yelled, "I am *not* the Catholic whore – *I* am the *Protestant* whore!")

In 1675 FitzRoy was created 1ˢᵗ Duke of Grafton and he and Isabella inherited Euston Hall when Arlington died in 1685. Partly demolished, attacked by fire and much modified since, but always magnificently re-built, the Hall and its grounds are today lovingly cared for by the 12ᵗʰ Duke of Grafton, who from time to time kindly opens his home to the public. A visit is highly recommended.

It is appropriate to conclude by mentioning that Arlington's money pot, Virginia was of course named after England's Virgin Queen, Elizabeth I, for in the preceding century – 1578 to be precise – she had spent three days at Euston as a guest of its then owner, Edward Rookwood. The Rookwoods were a Roman Catholic family and it is no exaggeration to say that Roman Catholics were at that time looked upon by the general population in much the same way as some people look suspiciously on all Muslims today. The Queen's visit, part of a royal progress through East Anglia, may have been designed to intimidate or trap Rookwood, for though Elizabeth tolerated Catholics who kept a low profile, she drew the line at overt 'Romish' or 'Papist' activity of any kind. It is undoubtedly not coincidental that she had with her a malevolent man called Richard Topcliffe, whom she employed to root out those Catholics who (for good reasons or otherwise) might be 'suspect'. Towards the end of the visit, the said Topcliffe dramatically claimed to have found an image of the Virgin Mary and equipment for celebrating Mass, which, Topcliffe claimed, had been hidden by Rookwood in a hay rick near the House. However, there are grounds for thinking that the offending items were 'planted' by Topcliffe himself. Be that the case or not, Elizabeth promptly ordered Rookwood to be incarcerated in Norwich Castle, where he was to languish for many years. However, it must be conceded in fairness that perhaps Topcliffe's antipathy to the Rookwoods was not entirely misplaced, for Edward Rookwood's cousin Ambrose was to become one of the famous or infamous Gunpowder Plot conspirators of 1605. (Ambrose's home, Coldham Hall, is at Stanningfield in Suffolk and is today owned by German supermodel Claudia Schiffer). The conspirators' intention was, of course, to blow up the Houses of Parliament with the King, the royal family and the whole of the British 'Establishment' of the day inside it. Had they succeeded, it is unlikely in the extreme that in the succeeding century George III would ever have become King.

And, of course, if George III had never become king, there might never have been an American Revolution . . .

SUFFOLK

The Birth of America's Legal System

"Americans accord Magna Carta semi-religious veneration, even greater reverence than the British, citing it constantly in political speeches, judicial opinions and newspaper opinion pieces as the symbol of the Rule of Law in the United States. If most of us know even a little of the Great Charter's history, we know that somehow it is the source of the liberties that we enjoy today. For America's founding fathers, Magna Carta symbolised the Rule of Law, *the precept that a government is bound by law in dealing with its people.* This view was set forth first in the Declaration of Independence, then in the state constitutions of the former thirteen colonies, and then in the Fifth and Fourteenth Amendments to the Federal Constitution." Thus wrote Ralph Turner, Emeritus Professor of History at the University of Florida, in the journal of the American Bar Association in 2003.

What is this Magna Carta? In essence, it symbolises and enshrines fundamental rights and liberties of an enduring nature. As Monty Python's Terry Jones narrated in a BBC documentary, it "may look like a plain, unassuming piece of parchment, but it's actually one of the most famous documents in the world. Magna Carta . . . has inspired people across the centuries, from Thomas Jefferson to Mahatma Gandhi."

The 'Great Charter' dates from the year 1215 (in reality a little earlier than that, as we shall see), a time when the barons of England were in dispute with King John, to whom the descriptive prefix 'Bad' is almost invariably attached. He was certainly a harsh collector of taxes, having inherited a near-empty treasury from his brother, Richard I. However, the money he collected so ruthlessly he unwisely spent recklessly, much of it in the unsuccessful prosecution of war in France, where he lost most of his French territories. This loss gave rise to another nickname, 'John Lackland'.

One of the few surviving copies of Magna Carta

Generally, King John's policies involved his desire to reduce the power of the barons and of the Church; both these pillars of the state naturally resented this deeply, especially as the manipulative King did not hesitate to employ against them methods which breached ancient rights and customs. The upshot was that King John soon became viewed as a man with little respect for the law of the land. Things came to a head in 1214 when King John mounted a massive and costly military campaign to re-conquer his lost territory of Normandy, a campaign for which he had imposed heavy taxes. The venture collapsed when he lost the Battle of Bouvines. Yet King John was undeterred and he pressured the barons to provide him with yet more money, which they were deeply reluctant to do. At this point, they began to concert a plan to bring the King back under control. At its heart was a desire to obtain a bill of rights which would specify what the monarch could and could not do and what the inalienable rights of his subjects were.

The seminal moment came in November 1214 when the Barons of England and the King gathered at the ancient Abbey of Bury St. Edmunds in Suffolk for a royal visit. The barons no doubt felt 'at home' at the Abbey, for the Abbot-elect, Hugh of Northwold, was widely perceived as a stern opponent of the King. Indeed, the Abbey's Sacrist, Robert of Gravely, issued a warning to the monarch in the following terms (as translated by R. M .Thomson): "My Lord King, this man assisting you and conducting himself as abbot-elect, is working with might and main to deprive you of your royal crown. And unless he is quickly persuaded by the royal provision [followers] to abandon this wicked idea, it is to be feared that within a short time he will accomplish what he has already set in motion against the royal dignity". This tip-off to the King may well have been motivated by the fact that Robert was an embittered man, having lost to Hugh in the election for the abbacy despite having confidently expected to win. Hugh in turn accused Robert of "cunning and falsity" in giving such a warning but his denial was itself false, for in truth Robert's warning was well-justified. In any event, it was at Bury St. Edmunds that, momentously, the barons 'got the bit between their teeth' and (known or unknown to the King) assembled at the most sacred spot in the whole abbey, the tomb of St. Edmund the Martyr, whose honoured burial in the town is reflected in its very name.

A monk called Roger of Wendover has left us a description of what happened next: ". . . commencing with those of the highest rank they [the barons] all swore that if the king refused to grant these liberties and laws, they themselves would withdraw from their allegiance to him and make war on him till he should, by a charter under his own seal, confirm to them everything they required. And firmly it was unanimously agreed that after Christmas they should all go together to the King and demand the confirmation of the aforesaid liberties to them, and that in the meantime they should prepare themselves with horses and arms so that if the King should endeavour to depart from his oath, they might by taking his castles compel him to satisfy their demands; and having arranged this, each man returned home."

The Magna Carta memorial at Bury St. Edmunds Abbey

This gathering of the barons and the historic oath they took in Suffolk some 800 years ago is now marked in the old Abbey by a commemorative plaque (though sadly, the building itself is largely ruinous). They barons promptly kept the sacred oath they had sworn at St. Edmund's tomb to initiate action immediately after Christmas, and in January 1215 conferred again with the King at the Temple in London. There they presented him with their draft charter but the monarch still wriggled. By May, the country was in a state of civil war and on the 17th of the month the barons seized London and thereby put the King in an extremely precarious position. Finally recognising that he was facing an unstoppable resolve, on June 15th he and the barons gathered in a meadow called Runnymede on the banks of the Thames. Here he finally accepted the 63-clause document. The most important of the clauses is the one which provided that no man could be arrested, imprisoned or have his possessions taken from him "except by the lawful judgement of his equals or by the law of the land". This clause underpins the principles of freedom from despotism and of trial by jury, the two sacred tenets of the English and American legal systems. So sacred do the Americans regard what happened at Runnymede, that in 1957 the American Bar Association erected a noble memorial marking the historic location. It is situated in a grassy enclosure on the lower slopes of Cooper's Hill, its classical dome shielding a pillar of English granite on which is inscribed, "To commemorate Magna Carta, symbol of Freedom Under Law".

The Magna Carta memorial at Runnymede,
erected by the American Bar Asssociation

To this day the American Bar Association continues to make pilgrimages to the revered spot. On 15th July 2000, to mark Millenium Year, the Association inscribed one of the memorial's flagstones with these words:

THE AMERICAN BAR ASSOCIATION RETURNS THIS DAY TO CELEBRATE MAGNA CARTA FOUNDATION OF THE RULE OF LAW FOR AGES PAST AND FOR THE NEW MILLENIUM

In conclusion, we can truly say that without Runnymede there would have been no foundation for the legal system which the English people transplanted to the New World. And the people of Suffolk can truly say that without Bury St. Edmunds there would have been no Runnymede . . .

SUFFOLK

George Washington's British Second-in-Command

Shakespeare famously wrote of a young boy with "shining morning face, creeping like a snail unwillingly to school". By contrast, we can be sure that in the year 1745 fourteen-year-old Charles Lee made his way not merely willingly but eagerly to his first day at Bury St. Edmunds Grammar School, for Lee was a bright lad, keen on cramming his head with knowledge. His parents hailed from Cheshire but had selected for him this well-respected place of learning in Suffolk because his uncle (his mother's brother, the Reverend William Bunbury) lived not far away in Mildenhall and was thus well-positioned to keep an eye on his nephew's welfare. At the Grammar School (and later at an academy in Switzerland) the young Lee had little difficulty in mastering Greek, Latin, French, Spanish, Italian and German. And in doing so he acquired a habit of scholarship which he was to retain all his life.

Lee was the son of the Colonel of the 55th Regiment of Foot and so it is perhaps not surprising that even as a youngster he nourished military ambitions; but he surely could not have foreseen that one day, having achieved prominence in the British Army, he would abandon that army, his comrades and his homeland in order to serve, instead, as a general in the army of the rebellious colonists in America. Neither could he have foreseen that in the Battle of Monmouth in 1778 he would suffer defeat at the hands of the British Commander-in-Chief Lord Cornwallis, whose family home of Culford Hall lay but a mile or two distant from his Bury St. Edmund's school. (See the chapter 'The American Revolution and the Reluctant British General'.)

After completing his education, Lee was commissioned as an ensign in his father's regiment (no doubt his father purchased the commission for him). He was a tall man, slim and bony and with a nose remarkable for its excessive size – he was to acquire the army nickname 'Naso'. To his intelligence and love of learning he added courage and a strong will but he was marked, too, by what some considered excessive ambition and vanity. There seems also to have been quarrelsome and sometimes erratic elements in his make-up – he was quick to take offence and fought several duels. His first posting was to uneventful garrison duties in Ireland. Active service soldiering began for him in 1754 when his regiment was sent to America for front-line operations in the French and Indian War. The conflict constituted a deeply serious threat to the colonists, for they faced possible total and permanent subjection to France and its Native American allies. In short, the hold of the British on their North American territories was in danger of being wholly broken. Lee saw much action: he served in the campaigns against Fort Duquesne, Louisburg and Fort Ticonderoga, in which latter affair he was severely wounded and spent a lengthy period of recuperation in hospital on Long Island. Restored to health, he participated in the capture of Fort Niagara and the classic victory over the French at Montreal, following which British sovereignty was extended over the whole of Canada.

Bury St. Edmunds Grammar School was housed in this building in Northgate Street when Charles Lee was a pupil

Of course, it was not only the French who recruited Native Americans as allies in this seven-year conflict – the British did too – and Lee developed some close connections with them. Indeed, one connection could not have been more intimate, for he married the daughter of White Thunder, a Seneca chief, and the couple became the parents of twins. The tribe assigned him the name 'Boiling Water' – possibly in reference to his turbulent personality.

Lee came home to England in 1761, at which time he attained the rank of major. (It is not recorded that his wife or children came to England with him; probably they did not, and the marriage perhaps ought to be regarded as a wartime dalliance.) However, with the reduction in hostilities his regiment was disbanded and he was retired on half pay. For the next ten years or so he led a colourful and varied existence, amongst other things going overseas to fight again, this time in foreign armies, principally for the Poles - who valued him highly and granted him the rank of Major General - and for the Portugese, Britain's oldest ally. Lee also travelled a great deal, at one point only just escaping a freezing death in the snow-swept Balkan mountains and a violent one in a major earthquake in Turkey. But he still felt undervalued in his homeland. Despite receiving an increase in his half-pay rank to Lieutenant Colonel in recognition of the indirect services he had rendered it by aiding friendly countries, it rankled that he was not accorded greater acclaim.

The most important point about this decade of his life, however, was his increasing disenchantment with the British Government's Tory beliefs. Lee had always had Whig leanings – that is to say, the belief that the consent of the people was the only legitimate source of power and that if the monarch failed them, the people had a right to resist. He denounced King George III as a "dolt" who was destroying English liberty. The upshot of all this was his decision in 1773 to up sticks and settle in America, arriving there at just in time for the famous protest against tea duties, the Boston Tea Party. In America, of course, Lee's republican views were welcomed with open arms and he spent most of the following year meeting prominent colonists such as George Washington, Patrick Henry and John Adams. Like

Tom Paine [10] (who hailed from Thetford, the small town a short horse-ride from Lee's old grammar school in Bury St. Edmunds), Lee put pen to paper in the cause of American independence, publishing two pamphlets, one of them attempting to persuade colonists that it was not entirely hopeless to fight against the might of the British Army. He would, he said, himself help to organise the colonists and to this end he wrote military manuals, trained troops and directed the construction of fortifications in Newport, Rhode Island and in New York. The Dictionary of American National Biography records that he performed these tasks 'brilliantly'.

General Charles Lee, showing the prominent nose which led to his British Army nickname of 'Naso'

10   Please see the chapter *Tom Paine, Revolutionary Propagandist and Namer of "The United States of America"*

By the spring of 1775 Lee was so committed to supporting rebellion that he bought a large tract of land in the Shenandoah Valley, thereby proving to the colonists, he said, that they could trust him implicitly, for now his future was intimately bound in with theirs. His choice of the Shenandoah Valley was almost certainly influenced by the fact that his friend Horatio Gates lived nearby. Gates was yet another Englishman, a Londoner and like Lee a former British Army officer-turned-revolutionary. They had fought alongside each other in the French and Indian Wars and in which Gates, though close enough to the action to have been severely wounded, had demonstrated an especial talent for military administration.

In June 1775 Lee, by now aged 45, was commissioned as the second major-general in the Continental Army (Washington being the first) and appointed deputy Commander-in-Chief. At the same time, seemingly being a man not disposed to take excessive financial risks, Lee solicited an undertaking that should the British Government deprive him of his landholdings in England, he would be fully compensated by Congress. Eager for his services, Congress readily agreed, some members believing he was more talented than Washington. In February 1776 Lee was given command of the Southern Military District which encompassed colonies from Virginia to Georgia, and in June repulsed a British assault on Fort Moultrie. A few weeks later he rejoined Washington in New York to take charge of the Continental Army's left wing. Things at this time were not going well for Washington: the British had forced him to retreat from Manhattan and then defeated him at the Battle of White Plains. Lee now felt that Washington should perform a tactical retreat from Fort Washington too (which the British had temporarily by-passed in their Manhattan advance), and he lobbied the Commander-in-Chief accordingly. Possibly influenced by the fact that his name was attached to the fort and that personal prestige was therefore at stake, Washington ignored the advice, only for Lee to be proved correct when the fort fell to the British with the loss of 3,000 men and enormous quantities of supplies. This was the first of more than one testy dispute between Lee and Washington, and Lee's confidence in Washington began to erode.

At this point something happened to Lee which was devastating and comic at one and the same time. To explain, we must first introduce a dashing young British cavalry officer named Banestre Tarlton. Tarlton had been a wild youth and at the age of 19 had squandered an inheritance of £5,000 (at least £500,000 in today's terms) in less than a year, spending it mainly on women and gambling at the Cocoa Tree Club in London. When he had heard that General Lee had abandoned the British Army and pledged allegiance to American independence, Tarlton had sworn to his fellow club members that one day he would track down the treasonous Lee and kill him.

Banastere Tarlton, General Lee's captor: portrait by Sir Joshua Reynolds

Thus motivated, and at the same time short of ready cash, Tarlton joined the 1st Dragoon Guards and sailed for America. There he displayed a mastery of horsemanship and an outstanding talent for leading men, gaining many victories and suffering few defeats. At the same time, he established a reputation among the rebels for excessive harshness, though it is doubtful that he was ever as brutal as claimed in some Hollywoood-style versions of history. For example, he maintained to the end of his life that in a notorious incident in which his force of American Loyalists and British regulars of the King's American Legion fired on and bayonetted rebel prisoners, killing a large number, no deliberate massacre was ever intended. His horse, Tarlton asserted – and numerous witnesses agreed – had been shot from under him and his enraged men, believing one of the surrendered troops had fired at their commander against the laws of war, attacked the prisoners on their own initiative. But that Banestre Tarlton did not favour excessive moderation is certainly true, for he criticised Lord Cornwallis for methods too mild. Mildness, wrote Tarlton, "does not reconcile enemies, but . . . discourages friends". He was a man of flamboyant and intimidating gestures, too, once riding his horse up a majestic staircase when capturing the colonial mansion of Carter's Grove in Virginia, bellowing threats and hacking at the handrail with his sabre as he did so. (The cuts in the handrail are still there today, which seems very appropriate as Tarlton's first name was pronounced 'bannister'.) But we must return from these wider points about Tarlton and revert to the first few months of his time in America and his relevance to General Lee.

Towards the end of 1776 George Washington was struggling across New Jersey at the head of an army which had suffered staggering losses and was now beset by large-scale desertion. His faith in Washington reduced to a new low, Lee became increasingly tardy in obeying the Commander-in-Chief's orders. Furthermore, he instructed his fellow rebel Briton, General Horatio Gates, who was battling through deep snow at the head of seven Continental regiments in a heroic attempt to go to Washington's aid, to transfer three of those regiments to his (Lee's) own command. Lee explained that he had plans to reconquer the Jerseys himself. On December 12th

Lee decided to spend the night at Widow White's Tavern at Basking Ridge, New Jersey, four miles behind the rebel lines. This apparently insignificant decision was to frustrate Lee's plans and cost him his freedom, for a Loyalist observed him there and communicated that fact to the British. In the morning Lee was slow to emerge from bed. Appearing downstairs at 8 o'clock, he was still half-dressed and apparently feeling somewhat lethargic, for he lounged around until about 10 o'clock, when he sat down for breakfast. He then wrote a letter to Horatio Gates in which he said "a certain great man" – meaning Washington – "is most damnably deficient". As Lee finished his letter, an aide called Major James Wilkinson casually looked out of the window and was staggered to see British dragoons coming round a corner at full charge.

And at the head of those dragoons was no other than Banestre Tarlton, 3,500 miles distant from the Cocoa Tree Club in London . . .

"Here, sir, are the British cavalry", Wilkinson yelled. "Where?" asked Lee. "Around the house." "Where is the guard? Why don't they fire? Do, Sir, see what has become of the guard", Lee ordered. Wilkinson recorded, "I passed into a room at the opposite end of the house, where I had seen the guard in the morning. Here I discovered their arms but the men were absent. I stepped out of the door and perceived the dragoons chasing them in different directions".

A little earlier that morning Tarlton had been about a mile away from the tavern when he had captured two Americans guarding the road to Morristown and a courier carrying orders to some of Lee's troops. Under threat of death, the American courier led Tarlton and his men to Widow White and her eminent guest. The lady of the house offered (rather optimistically, one feels) to hide Lee under a mattress, a humiliation he rejected. Mistress White then fled outside and pleaded with Tarlton not to kill her. He re-assured her he had no intention of doing so but said he was certain Lee was inside. Firing two shots through the front door, Tarlton gave a shouted warning that unless the remaining occupants surrendered he would set fire to the building and put them to the sword. Deciding as the well-known phrase has it that "discretion is the better part of valour", the Americans gave up.

Dishevelled and half-dressed, still partly in night-attire, Lee presented an undignified sight as he emerged and presented himself to the delighted Tarlton and his men. As a sensible soldier, Tarlton did not fulfil his oath to kill Lee, recognising that in reality the general was a hugely valuable asset as a prisoner and potential source of important military intelligence. Instead, partially-dressed and unkempt as Lee still was, Tarlton despatched him under heavy guard for interrogation at the headquarters of General Howe in New York.

When news of Lee's capture reached George Washington, he commented: "Unhappy man. Taken by his own imprudence." At the same time, in the light of Lee's recent lackadaisical approach to complying with instructions, Washington might well have allowed himself a brief smile at his subordinate's ironic fate. But more than a brief smile it was probably not, for Washington – as we shall see – retained substantial faith in Lee's military abilities, and it seems that (though annoyed) he decided to condone Lee's recent recalcitrance as simply based on a difference of view held in good faith. More widely, Lee's capture was greeted by the Continentals with dismay. One American summed up the public reaction thus: "The capture of General Lee, at so critical a moment in public affairs, was deeply deplored by the army and the whole country. Aside from the mortification of losing the second officer of the army in such a manner, the zeal with which he had embraced and sustained the American cause had won the affections of the people; and his military reputation, especially his recent successes in the south, had confirmed their good opinion and raised extravagant expectations of his future services."

Unsurprisingly, the British were inclined to treat Lee as a deserter and traitor and their initial intention was to send him to London for court martial. But the legal position was clear: Lee had resigned from his half-pay rank in the British Army prior to joining the American Army and the charges could not be sustained in law. In any event George Washington, keen to get Lee back, almost immediately started making overtures about a prisoner exchange. Washington opened the bartering by offering to swap Lee for five

German officers captured by the Americans whilst in British service but a deal was not concluded until eighteen months' later. When in May 1778 Lee was finally released, he rejoined the Continentals at Valley Forge and resumed his former status as Washington's second-in-command.

By this time, of course, the British had been able to interrogate Lee in depth and a document which came to light nearly a hundred years' later suggests that under pressure he *might* have been helpful to his former comrades to the extent of drafting a plan designed to ensure the rebels' defeat. But even if true, this could have been a piece of double-bluff, designed to lead the British astray; Lee was a clever man and deviousness was not foreign to his nature.

At a council of war shortly after rejoining the Continentals, Lee cautioned against a head-on attack against the British Army. His opinion found favour with the majority of senior officers and accordingly Washington adopted a cautious stance. But when British forces commenced a tactical retreat from Philadelphia, the American C-in-C espied an opportunity to conduct a major harassing attack on their rear and flanks. Lee was chosen to head the American force and on 28th June 1778 the two armies engaged each other in the Battle of Monmouth. His British opposite number was General Sir Henry Clinton. The battle was fought in intense heat with a high of over 37.8 degrees C (100 degrees F) and on both sides heat stroke was reckoned to have cost more lives than musket- and cannon-fire. Lee launched his attack on the British rearguard commanded by General Cornwallis (he who been Lee's near neighbour when a teenager in Bury St. Edmunds). Things began to go awry for Lee very early on when Cornwallis brought up hidden reinforcements and one of Lee's subordinates moved his men out of a wood without orders. After several hours of fighting under the scorching sun, several American units began to retreat and soon the retreat turned into a general rout. Whatever the rights and wrongs of his orders, Lee failed to get a grip on the situation. Washington was appalled and arrived to take personal command, sending Lee to the rear after an exchange of words as heated as the Monmouth County air. Washington then saved the day by rallying the disheartened and disorganised rebel troops and counter-attacking but was unable to prevent the British from achieving their wider aim of making their way to Sandy Hook and thence by water to New York, taking all their supplies with them.

The affair at Monmouth brought about the ruin of General Lee. Washington was in no forgiving mood this time, laying responsibility firmly on his second-in-command and ordering a court martial. The court martial took place in the village inn at Englishtown and Lee was found guilty. His punishment was to be relieved of his command for one year. The verdict was endorsed by the Continental Congress but the vote was close, suggesting that many still retained their faith in this charismatic man. However, when Lee wrote a letter of protest to Congress, he was informed that Congress no longer had need of his services – surely the only outcome which Lee could realistically have expected.

After Congress's final rejection, Lee for two or three months lingered in Philadelphia but then removed to his estate in Berkeley County. It is recorded that there "he lived more like a hermit than a citizen of the world or the member of a civilised community. His house was little more than a shell, without partitions, and containing scarcely the necessary articles of furniture for the most common uses. To a gentleman who visited him in this forlorn retreat, where he found a kitchen in one corner, a bed in another, books in a third, saddles and harness in a fourth, Lee said, 'Sir, it is the most convenient and economical establishment in the world. The lines of chalk, which you see on the floor, mark the divisions of the apartments and I can sit in any corner, and give orders, and overlook the whole, without moving from my chair'."

Ultimately feeling disenchantment with his new country and disappointed with his life, Lee wrote in his will: "I desire most earnestly that I may not be buried in any church or churchyard, or within a mile of any Presbyterian or Anabaptist meeting house; for since I have resided in this country I have kept so much bad company when living that I do not choose to continue it when dead."

Lee died at the early age of fifty in 1782. He was visiting Philadelphia at the time, where, presumably to his eternal disgust, he lies buried in Christ Church churchyard.

SUFFOLK

1676: The First American Rebel

One hundred years before the Declaration of Independence, a heated rebellion broke out in the first successful English settlement of Jamestown and in the wider colony of Virginia. Independence from the Mother Country featured not at all in the dispute but the questioning of established authority certainly did, for the objective was the overthrow of the colony's governor, Sir William Berkeley. Rebellion, it seems, was in the genes of many English settlers and, of course, was ultimately to manifest itself in the American Revolution. The leader of the Virginia rebellion – the first-ever in British America – was Nathaniel Bacon, born in 1647 and the son of Sir Thomas Bacon of Friston Hall, Saxmundham, Suffolk. The Bacons were a notable family and boasted numerous prominent ancestors and contemporaries, amongst them Sir Nicholas Bacon, the Keeper of the Great Seal for Elizabeth I, and Francis Bacon, the statesman, illustrious philosopher and scientist.

Nathaniel graduated from Cambridge University with an M.A. in 1667 and his life soon acquired a turbulence which was seldom to leave it, for within three years he was to marry a woman called Elizabeth Duke in the face of strong objections from his own father and her parents. Elizabeth was disinherited by her family and Nathaniel was himself without sufficient means to support married life, especially after his wife gave birth to their two daughters. Desperate and reckless, he gave way to temptation and dabbled in land fraud and, though escaping prison, suffered entanglement in a lengthy court case. His father ran out of patience with him and decided that to part with money to establish his son in the New World was less objectionable that to tolerate his remaining in the Old and incurring the risk of his further tarnishing the family name. Armed with his father's surprisingly generous subvention of £1,800

– equivalent to £200,000 or more today – Bacon and his little flock arrived in Virginia in 1674. In addition to bringing money, he had the advantage of family connections there, for he was related to Frances, wife of Virginia's governor, Sir William Berkeley; moreover, a cousin, another Nathaniel, sat on Virginia's Council of State. 'Our' Nathaniel's money and connections plus his undisputed drive and intelligence led within a twelve-month to him, too, obtaining a seat on the Council. All in all, one might have thought that a man lucky enough to have escaped a fraud case in England and a chronic shortage of cash would at this point have blessed his good luck, rested on his laurels and spent time consolidating his position.

Se ipso pinxit.   *T. Cha.*

S.ʳ NATHANIEL BACON.
From an Original at the Lord Viscount Grimston's, at Gorhambury.

But no, Nathaniel, being a man of some ego, recklessness and restlessness, soon began to openly support a number of longer-established English colonists in their opposition to the Governor's policies. At issue were some questions of taxation (surprise, surprise) but the crucial point was the Governor's policy towards the Native Americans. Some of the so-called 'Red Indians' were friendly but many were understandably not and the colonists had suffered some brutal deaths at the latter's hands. Berkeley believed that the way to deal with the problem was to contain it by building a chain of defensive forts but many of the colonists thought the plan too expensive and, more importantly, lacking in ambition. Their view was that nothing would suffice except an aggressive campaign to take the war to the enemy and punish him hard. (Some suspected that Berkeley wanted to conciliate the Native Americans to protect his profits from his fur-trading links with them.) At about this point, the Native Americans launched a new offensive. Bacon, his charisma having established him as a leading settler, organised a retaliatory attack (after inflaming himself and his adherents with a generous dose of brandy) and, amongst other things, descended on a 'Red Indian' village and killed most of the inhabitants – men, women and children alike.

Following his return to Jamestown after this first and unauthorised punitive expedition, Bacon confronted the Governor and demanded a commission in the Militia. Berkeley turned him down flat, whereupon Bacon instructed some of his men to level their muskets at Berkeley's chest. The courageous Governor showed his mettle by "baring his breast" and challenging Bacon to fire a fatal shot himself. Bacon backed down, which must have humiliated him more than a little but hindered him not at all his determination to continue his campaign against the indigenous peoples. This he promptly set about doing. Not untypically, though, he immediately marred matters by launching a raid on the one local tribe that was friendly, the Pamunkies. The Pamunkies had in fact been in the process of supplying warriors to help the colonists against an unfriendly tribe at the very time Bacon was threatening to shoot the Governor!

Bacon's campaign lasted several months during which he pursued his aggressive policy vigorously. But the passage of time did nothing to relieve his feelings of enmity to Berkeley – in fact, it buttressed his conviction that Virginia would be a better place if he, Bacon, 'called the shots' both literally and metaphorically. In this belief, he entered Jamestown with several hundred of his men and burned much of Virginia's modest capital to the ground. What Bacon hoped to achieve by this is not clear, but his decision to wreck what was already an historic little town suggests his mind was dominated by an irrational destructiveness and a desire to demonstrate his personal power.

Sir William Berkeley had not, of course, stood idly by during Bacon's maraudings, but had mustered official forces and called in an English naval squadron to support them. Bacon was forced to retreat across the James River but for him there was to be no so-called 'glorious end' fighting to the death: instead, he caught dysentery and died lingeringly and painfully. Deprived of their leader, his followers were unable to withstand a series of amphibious attacks across the river; the captain of one of the Royal Navy ships, Thomas Graham, successfully, though dishonourably, finally subdued the rebels with the assurance that they would be pardoned if they surrendered – but once in his ship's hold he trained his guns on them and made them prisoners . . .

Berkeley re-established his and the Crown's authority by confiscating the land and assets of the leading rebels and publicly hanging twenty-three of them. In England, the story went that the King, Charles II, himself entertained doubts about his colonial governor, allegedly stating, "That old fool has put to death more people in that naked country than I did here for the murder of my father".

Who can now establish the exact rights and wrongs of all this? Probably no-one unless more information comes to light. But one thing is certain: the internecine feud did nothing to advance the progress of the English in the New World. The Governor's wife, Lady Berkeley, was one of many who suffered by it all. She wrote to a cousin that on her return to it, her house "looked like one of those the boys pull down at Shrovetide, and [took] almost as much to repair as if it had been new to build, and no sign that ever there had been a fence round it." Such is often the fate of women: men destroy and it is women who are left to put things back together again . . .

SUFFOLK

The American Revolution and the Reluctant British General

It is inconceivable to us in the 21st century that a man could be a General in the British Army and, simultaneously, a Member of Parliament. But let us suspend disbelief for a moment and suppose it possible: could we then go on to envisage that man also supporting a Government composed of his bitter political opponents? And fighting for that Government in a war it had declared against fellow British citizens for whom he had deep sympathy? The answers must surely be no, no and no. And yet this is precisely what happened in the case of General Lord Charles Cornwallis in the American War of Independence.

Let us begin at the beginning.

Cornwallis's family seat was at Culford Park in Suffolk, just a mile or two from the ancient town of Bury St. Edmunds (where General Charles Lee, the English schoolboy who later became George Washington's deputy Commander-in-Chief, attended Grammar School). [11] Cornwallis was born on the last day of 1738, the eldest son of the first Earl Cornwallis and his wife Elizabeth who, incidentally, gave birth to him whilst in a townhouse in Grosvenor Square, London – ironically, the current location of the United States' Embassy. As a child and youth, Cornwallis followed a traditional educational path for the titled and wealthy, first attending Eton College at Windsor and then Clare College at Cambridge University. At age nineteen he embarked on his army career as an ensign in the Grenadier Guards and at twenty-two on his political career, being elected – virtually as of right – as Member of Parliament for another Suffolk town, Eye, where his family had been prominent for centuries. This twin path

---

11   See the chapter *George Washington's British Second-in-Command*

and its inherent conflicts of interest raised not an eyebrow, for at that time men of Cornwallis's class were born – were they not? – to rule in any capacity or combination of capacities they cared to select.

Culford Park, the Suffolk home of General Cornwallis

Cornwallis's knowledge of military matters having been enhanced by study at a military academy in Turin in Italy, he went on to fight during the 1760s in a number of British Army campaigns in mainland Europe. During this period, his father died and thus the younger man inherited Culford Park and, of course, much else. In the House of Commons, he supported the Whigs, a reforming party which in the 19th century was to re-brand itself as the Liberals. Of great importance to his story is the fact that the Whigs were highly sympathetic to the British colonists in America and opposed the Stamp Act of 1765, by which the British Parliament required the colonists to pay – for the first time – a directly-levied internal tax. This took the form of an impost on every piece of paper the colonists used, from legal documents to playing cards. Unsurprisingly, given his sympathies, Cornwallis voted against the tax but a majority of MPs were in favour and so it became law. The colonists were much put out, arguing that only their own representative assemblies had the right to tax them. This was the origin of the famous, or infamous, "no taxation without representation" dispute, which, of course, was the trigger for the war that was to break out between mother and daughter countries a decade later.

It was unavailing for the British Parliament to argue, as it did, that the colonists were morally bound to make a contribution to the large debts the home country had incurred in sending an army to America to defend them against the French in the Seven Years' War; as the colonists saw it, they had spent substantial sums on maintaining their own militias during the period of hostilities, and simply did not want to 'cough up' more to offset the mother country's costs. Mob violence in the thirteen colonies ensued and the British Parliament deemed it prudent to revoke the Act the following year. But Parliament was determined not to let the matter drop and soon came back with a further series of taxation measures which, unsurprisingly, proved equally unwelcome. Collectively, these acts were known as the Townshend Acts, after Charles Townshend, the British Chancellor of the Exchequer, whose family seat was Raynham Hall in Norfolk (which remains in the hands of the Townshend family to this day). This must have been a matter of personal regret and some embarrassment to Cornwallis, for his mother was herself a member of the Townshend family! These Townshend taxes, too, were soon withdrawn in the face of renewed opposition until only the tax on tea remained. But, collectively, the Stamp Act and the Townshend Acts had already soured relations to the extent of causing long-term damage, to be exemplified most notably by the Boston Tea Party of 1773.

At the onset of open hostilities in 1775, Cornwallis, by now a 37-year-old major-general, was appointed by King George III to take seven regiments of infantry to America to support the British commander there, Sir William (later Lord) Howe. On the face of it, this was very surprising, for the King detested Whigs and was acutely aware that Cornwallis, as a prominent Whig, had worked against the very measures which had inspired His Majesty's British subjects in America to revolt. The King, though wishing the young major-general to put his military talents at his disposal, must have wondered, "Can Cornwallis be trusted?" And Cornwallis, sympathetic to the colonists as he was, must have pondered, "Should I resign?" But the necessary order was both given and obeyed. The reason for the obedience lies in one thing: the personal loyalty to the monarchy displayed over centuries by generation upon generation of the Cornwallis family. In a nutshell, Charles Cornwallis – as the King would have been well aware – was profoundly reluctant to break his family's hallowed tradition of service to the Crown; had he done so, he would have brought on himself and his bloodline the stain of historic dishonour. So, in 1776, off to North America he went.

Raynham Hall, East Raynham, Norfolk:
family home of Charles Townshend

Once there, Cornwallis scored a number of victories and soon took a leading part in chasing George Washington and his army from out of New York and all of New Jersey. In 1777 he was largely responsible for another notable victory over Washington, at the Battle of Brandywine in Pennsylvania. Unfortunately, towards the end of 1778 Cornwallis received news that his wife was very ill. He briefly returned to England and was at her bedside when she died in February 1779. Despite this blow, he resumed his services to the King and by August was back in New York. From there he went to South Carolina and in 1780 defeated the larger rebel forces of General Horatio Gates at the Battle of Camden. (Gates, be it noted, was another Englishman, a Londoner. Perhaps we can detect here, as in many other instances, the characteristics of civil war, a fact that seems to have been acknowledged by the colonists and their successors by their use of the terms 'American Revolution' and 'Revolutionary War' as opposed to the British view of the conflict as 'the War of Independence'.) In 1781, again in the face of a much larger rebel force which inflicted heavy casualties on his men, Cornwallis defeated Major General Nathaniel Greene at the Battle of Guilford Court House in North Carolina. (It is fair to state that Cornwallis's own guns caused many of the British casualties, for he ordered them to fire grapeshot into the mixed mass of battle; this rattled the British less than the Americans, who broke and ran. Ruthless, but effective.)

Clearly, Cornwallis was a man of much determination and military talent. But his efforts need to be put into the context of the first two British commanders-in-chief, Sir William Howe and Sir Henry Clinton. The former has received much criticism, at the time and since, for not taking decisive steps during his time in command to ensure that Washington's numerous failures were not turned into strategic defeat. But we should note that Howe, like Cornwallis, was also a prominent Whig and enjoyed very many friendly associations with Americans. He may thus have been appointed commander-in-chief partly in hope of his achieving a measure of conciliation – or at least lessening the bitterness of the conflict. This may have led him on occasions to consciously take decisions not to exploit his successes to the full, for which – we can say in hindsight – he can be condemned as naïve. So one must take a view: was Howe an incompetent ditherer or did he sometimes hold back through a misplaced belief that the colonists, having been taught some stiff lessons, would seek some sort of settlement?

Now to Sir Henry Clinton, Howe's successor: we do not need to consider his record in any depth, it sufficing to say that after the Battle of Guilford Court House Cornwallis moved up to Virginia, where Clinton issued him with a number of "confusing, contradictory and not entirely forceful orders". Eventually he received a firm instruction from Clinton to make his way to the coast at Yorktown and to establish there a fortified post to shelter ships in anticipation of the arrival of the Royal Navy. These British vessels, Clinton intended, would provide Cornwallis with re-inforcements and supplies. But alas for the British! – everything was to go wrong. In fact, the move to Yorktown was to prove the mother country's worst decision of the whole war and, de facto, bring about the loss of all thirteen of her American colonies.

France was at the heart of the disaster, for by now she had been actively engaged on the colonists' side for a considerable time and was providing large numbers of troops and powerful naval forces. To stress the ironic nature of this Franco-American alliance is hardly necessary, for – as noted earlier – the trigger for the Americans' revolt had been the taxes sought by Britain to recoup some of the money it had spent protecting those very same Americans *against* France. Had that struggle been unsuccessful, the colonists, to their horror, would have fallen completely under French rule.

But now – "Stone the crows!" as the English say – the British faced a situation in which the colonists had recruited their former bitter enemy as their ally in a war against their former British defender! And this, be it repeated, in a war ignited by a wrangle over costs incurred in fighting a France which until recently had been the enemy of both! Modern American friends and readers might perhaps forgive the remark that the charges of hypocrisy levelled by the British against the colonists at the time were not without merit . . .

Be all that as it may, in accordance with Clinton's orders, Cornwallis and his 8,000 men – half of whom had become infected by malaria and were thus largely militarily ineffective – made their way to what was to be their doom on the Yorktown Peninsula. The 4,000 or so fit men hastily constructed defensive works but were acutely short of food and ammunition and well-outnumbered by the 8,000 French regulars and 8,000 American regulars, plus 3,000 American militia who soon followed, and established a siege. The Americans were commanded by Washington and the French by Comte de Rochambeau. Of supreme – indeed, critical – importance was the almost simultaneous arrival off the coast of an extremely powerful French battle fleet under Admiral de Grasse, fresh from defeating his outnumbered British opponent, Admiral Thomas Graves. (By this time the Royal Navy, dominant though it had been, was vastly over-extended). Cornwallis's force was thus placed in a deeply unenviable position, trapped between the 'devils' of Washington and de Rochambeau on the one side and the 'deep blue sea' of de Grasse on the other. Things became even more difficult for the British when yet another French force under Admiral Barras landed the French Army's siege artillery, much greater in quantity and power of shot than the artillery Cornwallis possessed. To put matters in a nutshell, after three weeks of more-or-less non-stop bombardment by day and night, Cornwallis reluctantly but rightly concluded that he had no alternative but to surrender.

Cornwallis, usually a man of considerable moral courage, was so temporarily lowered in spirit that he felt unable to face the formal surrender ceremony on October 19th. He gave his second-in-command, General Charles O'Hara, the unenviable task of attending in his place. In Cornwallis's absence, Washington absented himself too and similarly deputed attendance to his second-in-command, General Benjamin Lincoln, though for an entirely different reason: Lincoln had himself surrendered to Cornwallis at the Battle of Charleston the preceding year in the largest American surrender of the war, and Washington was generous enough to grant Lincoln a compensatory satisfaction. (Benjamin Lincoln, as his name suggests, was a descendant of the Lincoln family which had emigrated to the New World from Hingham in Norfolk, England and an ancestor of President Abraham Lincoln; ironically, Hingham lay only a few miles from Cornwallis's mansion at Culford, Suffolk.)[12]

---

12   See the chapter *General Benjamin Lincoln: You win some, you lose some . . .*

At the surrender ceremony the British drummers and fifers wryly played "The World Turned Upside Down", recognising Yorktown's profound significance, i.e. a defeat from which the British would be unable to recover. An American eyewitness, Dr. James Thatcher, recorded in his journal, however, that when it "came to the last act of the drama", grounding their arms, the spirit of the British soldier was put to the severest test: here the mortification could not be concealed . . . many of the soldiers manifested a sullen temper, throwing their arms on the pile with violence, as if determined to render them useless". (The ghosts of these men might have been a little consoled when, at a ceremony to mark the battle 100 years later in 1881, American President Chester Arthur generously ordered that the closure of the ceremony take the form of a salute to the British flag.)

When the news of the defeat finally reached the British Prime Minister, Lord North, far away in England, he exclaimed, "Oh, God, it's all over". Meanwhile, Cornwallis and his men were temporarily held prisoner, Cornwallis returning to Britain in January 1782. He retained the full confidence of George III and of the majority of the British people, the blame for Yorktown being placed by most on Clinton for having placed his subordinate – a man with many victories to his credit – in an impossible position. There was, however, what might be called a 'war of pamphlets' between the two men and their respective supporters and detractors. We can conclude that Cornwallis won this pamphlet battle, as he had so many real battles, because in 1786 he was appointed as Governor General of India, the brightest jewel in the British Empire's crown. There, despite unsurprisingly sharing some of the racist views of his time, he achieved a fine reputation for enlightened rule of its teeming Indian millions and for stamping out corruption in the British civil service and elite.

Between returning from America and departing for India, Cornwallis naturally spent a great deal of time at his residence of Culford Park in Suffolk, surely an idyllic setting in which to recover from the stresses and strains of years of warfare. Naturally, he entertained numerous guests, including on several occasions the Frenchman Francois de la Rochefoucauld, the noted author of memoirs and maxims. Rochefoucauld recorded in his book "A Frenchman's Year in Suffolk" that Cornwallis was "regarded as a most excellent man and the best of neighbours; the best of husbands and fathers; the respect people feel for him in the district is general". Rochefoucauld added that Cornwallis "showed me extraordinary kindness". This, Cornwallis explained, was in part because he had been treated so well by French officers when their prisoner after Yorktown and "wished to show his gratitude to all Frenchmen".

Cornwallis left the office of Governor General of India in 1793 but after making other distinguished contributions to British public service, returned to India to serve a second term in 1805. Sadly, he died shortly after his arrival. His impressive tomb is at Ghazipur, and is maintained by the Indian Government to this day in testimony not only to his being a great soldier but a good man. Which of us can hope to be remembered for more?

EPILOGUE

A trip to the *real* Washington (and it's *not* in the District of Columbia!)

George Washington, the founding father of the United States of America, was proud of his English ancestry. As described elsewhere within this book, he repeatedly referred to himself in his writings as a "true-born Englishman". He was, of course, of pure British blood and, for at least the first half of his life, an ardently loyal subject of the British Crown. Indeed, his praise for the monarchy was often fulsome: to quote but one example, in a letter to the Governor of Virginia in 1757 he wrote to express "the deep sense we have of His Majesty's great wisdom and paternal care for his colonies . . ." How things were to change! – for ultimately this "true-born" Englishman was to personify in the phases of his own life the transformation of the thirteen British colonies into a new and independent nation. In the first phase, he fought for and with the British in the North American component of the Seven Years' War; in the second, he experienced disenchantment with British rule; and in the third, he fought against the British in the American Revolution.

George Washington's immediate direct ancestors were from Essex, as the reader by now will know. But from where in England did the family *originate*? The answer is – from *the true and original* Washington, which existed long before its upstart imitator in the District of Columbia in the USA! The *real* Washington is a small village in the north-eastern English county of Tyne and Wear. It took its name from George Washington's ancestors, just as Washington D.C. took its name from him. Centred on the family's ancient residence, Washington Old Hall, the village of Washington retains to this day its ancient feel despite being cheek-by-jowl with modern development. The two-storey Hall, set back from a tree-lined road, is constructed of mellow sandstone and marvellously cared-for by the National Trust. It is, of course, a place of pilgrimage for Americans and has been for many a long year.

Washington Old Hall,
the ancestral family home of George Washington

Most of the Hall dates from the 1600s but the foundations, the west wall and parts of the kitchen go back to medieval times. The family lived in the Hall for five generations and it was from here that they spread to the county of Essex, from where the famous George's immediate ancestors departed for the New World.

About a dozen miles to the south of Washington is Durham Cathedral, of epic magnificence, and also significant for its connection with George's ancestor John Washington, who in about 1400 became Chancellor of the Cathedral and in 1416 its Prior. There is a movingly-worded plaque to commemorate John in the cloisters.

*The John Washington memorial plaque
in Durham Cathedral*

The family also had links with Lancashire and though well outside the geographical remit of this book, it must be mentioned that a trip there to visit Selby Abbey is well worth while, for in the 1400s a stained-glass copy of the Washington coat of arms was installed there. The visitor will immediately perceive that the flag of the District of Columbia, the home of the USA's capital, is taken from that ancient symbol and, more particularly, the theme of stars and stripes is incorporated in *the* Stars and Stripes.

*The Washington coat of arms in Selby Abbey
and on the flag of the District of Columbia*

Expressions of Thanks

SINCERE THANKS to **Doctor Meriel Overy** and **Mr. Andrew Ramsay** for, respectively, arranging and conducting for me a cataract operation which greatly facilitated the writing of this book

to **Denise Sharpe** at Elveden Courtyard for her always-cheerful help – and to all the other lovely people there!

to **Lester Bennett** of Printing for Pleasure for his invaluable help

and to my wife **Clare**, with thanks for everything and all my love, admiration and gratitude.

Bibliography/Sources

BOOKS and other source material I have consulted and to whose authors, still with us or long past, I am immensely grateful:

The Library of American Biography:
Jared Sparks: Harper & Bros. New York 1856

American Leaders & Heroes: W. F. Gordy:
Charles Scribner's Sons, New York 1907

The Founders: Charles K. Bolton:
The Boston Athaneum 1926

Life of George Washington:
Washington Irving: G.P. Putnam & Co., New York 1855

Every Day Life in the Massachusetts Bay Colony:
G.F. Dow: Boston 1935

The Parliamentary History of England:
T.C. Hansard 1813

A Brief & True Report of the New Found Land of Virginia:
Thomas Hariot: 1590

Sketches of the Rulers of India:
G.D. Oswell: Clarendon Press: Oxford 1908

The Memoirs of the late Charles Lee:
London 1792

The Treason of Charles Lee:
George H. Moore: Charles Scribner: New York 1890

The 13 Colonies of North America:
R.W. Jefferey: Methuen & Co.: London 1908

Journal of an American Prisoner in the War of 1812:
G.M.Fairchild: Quebec 1909

The Writings of George Washington (4 vols.):
Ed. J.C. Fitzpatrick.: 1931

Journals of George Washington:
Ed.R.Dinwiddie: 1893

Bartholomew Gosnold of Otley & America:
J. Haden etc.: Barny Books 2007

Admiral of New England:
J. Haden etc.: Barny Books 2005

Captain Christopher Newport:
J. Haden etc.: Barny Books 2006

Captain John Smith:
J. Haden etc.: Barny Books 2005

Those Damned Rebels:
Michael Pearson, De Capo Press 1972

The Mayflower of Harwich:
Paul H. Simmons, UK 2011

Campaigns of British Army, Washington & New Orleans 1814-15: G.R.Gleig

When Britain Burned the White House: Peter Snow:
John Murray, London 2013

Mr. & Mrs. Madison's War:
Hugh Howard: Bloomsbury Press: 2012

John Wesley and Marriage:
Bufford W. Coe: Lehigh University Press: 1996

The Heydey of Their Strength:
M.E.Lonsdale: Hingham: 1979

The Justice and Necessity of Taxing the American Colonies: Anon. London 1766

True to the Old Flag:
G.A. Henty

Captain Thomas Willoughby:
Alice Grand Walter, Virginia Beach 1978

Journal of an American Prisoner at Fort Malden & Quebec in War of 1812: James Reynolds

The Treason of Charles Lee:
George H. Moore New York 1858

The Beginners of a Nation:
Edward Eggleston, New York 1896

The Beginnings of the American Revolution:
Ellen Chase, New York 1910

Life of George Washington:
Washington Irving, New York 1855

Domestic life in Virginia in the 17th Century:
Annie Lash Jester, Williamsburg 1957

The Romantic story of the Mayflower Pilgrims:
A.C. Addison, Boston, Mass. 1910

New Discoveries at Jamestown:
John L. Cotter & Paul Hudson, U.S. Dept. of Interior 1957

Burke's Speech on Conciliation with America:
Edmund Burke 1775

The Colonisation of North America 1492-1783:
Eugene Bolton, Washington University 1920

History of Hingham, Norfolk, England:
Anon. East Dereham 1921

England in America 1580-1652:
Lyon Gardiner Taylor, New York 1904

The Women Who Came in the Mayflower:
Annie Russel Marble, Worcester, Mass. Date unknown.

The Puritans:
Perry Miller, New York 1963

The Mayflower and her Log:
Azel Ames, 1907

The Pilgrims of New England:
Mrs. J. B. Webb, unknown

The Birth of the Nation:
Sara A. Pryor, London 1907

Websites too numerous to mention, but deep gratitude is expressed by the author to all those who contribute *reliable* information to the internet.

ILLUSTRATIONS: ACKNOWLEDGED WITH GRATITUDE

Grand Union Flag:
Courtesy of U.S. Navy

Washington & Grand Union Flag:
Public Domain

Longstowe Hall:
© and courtesy of Michael Trolove: geographia.org.uk

Colchester Castle:
Courtesy of M. Barker

Emmanuel College, Cambridge:
Wiki Commons Unrestricted Licence

Harvard House, Stratford on Avon:
Wiki Commons Unrestricted Licence

Abraham Brown House, Watertown:
Public Domain, via courtesy of Digital Commonwealth

Christ's College, Cambridge:
© 'The Wub' & licensed for re-use under Creative commons

Thomas Nelson House, Yorktown:
Untraced

Trinity College, Cambridge:
Public Domain, courtesy of Hans Wolff

Groton Hall:
Author's photo

Castling's Hall:
Author's photo

Harley-Davidson Memorial:
Author's photo

Classic Image Harley Davidson:
Courtesy of 'Tuxlie', Wiki Creative Commons Licence

Earls Colne Priory:
© Robert Edwards & licensed for re-use under Creative Commons

John Carwardine as Union Officer:
Public Domain

Chigwell School:
© John Davies & licensed for re-use under Creative Commons

All Saints Church, Purleigh:
© Peter Stack & licensed for re-use under Creative Commons

St Nicholas, Little Braxted:
© John Salmon & licensed for re-use under Creative Commons

Christopher Jones' House:
Author's photo

Alma Inn, Harwich:
Author's photo

Replica of Mayflower:
© Kunal Mukherjee & licensed for re-use under Creative Commons

Timbers of the Mayflower Barn:
Public Domain

Cross Keys, Dagenham:
Untraced

Wright Flyer:
Public Domain

Pocahontas saving John Smith: Public Domain,
courtesy of the Architect of the Capitol, Washington DC

Heacham Manor: © Copyright Brian Chadwick
licensed for re-use under Creative Commons

Wattle and daub:
Untraced

Laxon-style house, Jamestown:
© Morgan Riley & licensed for re-use under creative Commons

Laxon-style house, Lincolnshire:
© Morgan Riley & licensed for re-use under Creative Commons

Epworth Rectory:
© David Wright & licensed for re-use under Creative Commons

Wesley Statue, Savannah:
Courtesy of Official Savannah Guide

William Coddington Portrait:
Public Domain

Scrooby Manor House:
Public Domain

St. Wilfred's Church, Scrooby:
© John Slater & licensed for re-use under Creative Commons

Gainsborough Old Hall:
© Chris Coleman & licensed for re-use under Creative Commons

St. Botolph's, Boston:
© Dave Hitchborne & licensed for re-use under Creative Commons

Boston Guildhall:
© Richard Croft & licensed for re-use under Creative Commons

Re-enactor at Guildhall:
Author's photograph

Otley Hall:
Author's photo

Bury St. Edmunds St Mary's Churchyard:
Geographia Creative Commons & Licencsed for re-use

Gibraltar Barracks, Bury St. Edmunds:
Untraced

44th Foot Re-enactment:
Untraced

Gutted Capitol, Washington:
Public Domain

White House in Flames:
Public Domain

Euston Hall, Suffolk:
©Ashley Dace & licensed for re-use under Creative Commons

Magna Carta:
Untraced

Magna Carta Memorial, Bury St. Edmunds:
© David Dixon 7 licensed for re-use under Creative Commons

Magna Carta Memorial, Runnymede:
© Len Williams & licensed for re-use under Crteative Commons

Bury St. Edmund's Grammar School, Northgate Street:
Untraced

General Charles Lee:
Public Domain/'Bing'-listed as Creative Commons

Banastre Tarlton:
Wikipedia

Sir Nathaniel Bacon:
Wikipedia

Culford Park:
© Bigfish 1982 & licensed for re-use as Creative Commons

Raynham Hall:
Author's photo

Washington Old Hall:
© P.J. Marriot & licensed for re-use under Creative Commons

Washington Memorial Plaque:
© Kaihsu Tai & licensed for re-use under Creative Commons

Washington Coat of Arms & Flag:
© Tomasz Steifer & licensed for re-use under Creative Commons

Back Cover:
Author's photos

SPECIAL NOTE

Any person who feels I have not adequately credited them, either in written source materials or illustrations, is cordially invited to contact me so that I may rectify the defect in any future edition(s). In the meantime, please accept my apologies (if any are due!)

By the same author

The Most Secret Place On Earth
The story of the East Anglian Village of Elveden
and the World's First Tanks
(Published by Larks Press)

"A great book"
– *BBC Radio East*

"Splendid"
– *Eastern Daily Press*

"A superb account, no frills, easily read,
fascinating and above all enjoyable"
– *Col. Stephen May, Regimental Colonel, Royal Tank Regiment*

"Fabulous"
– *Brigadier John Maxwell*

"Fills a huge gap in the known record
of the history of the early tanks"
– *Richard Pullen, author of "The Landships of Lincoln" etc.*

"A subject that reaches beyond local,
beyond even national import,
to claim its place in global military history"
– *Military History Monthly*

"A truly epic saga"
– *Steven Snelling, author of VCs of the First World War etc.*